Twayne's United States Authors Series

EDITOR OF THIS VOLUME

Kenneth Eble

University of Utah

James Norman Hall

TUSAS 323

James Norman Hall

JAMES NORMAN HALL

By ROBERT ROULSTON
Murray State University

TWAYNE PUBLISHERS
A DIVISION OF G. K. HALL & CO., BOSTON

Copyright © 1978 by G. K. Hall & Co.

Published in 1978 by Twayne Publishers,
A Division of G. K. Hall & Co.
All Rights Reserved

Printed on permanent/durable acid-free paper and bound
in the United States of America

First Printing

Library of Congress Cataloging in Publication Data

Roulston, Robert.
James Norman Hall.

(Twayne's United States authors series ; TUSAS 323)
Bibliography: p. 159 - 64
Includes index.
1.   Hall, James Norman, 1887 - 1951—Criticism and
interpretation.   I.   Title.
PS3515.A363Z83   813'.5'2   78-16623
ISBN 0-8057-7255-3

Contents

About the Author

Robert Roulston was born on May 27, 1930, in Baltimore, Maryland. After attending public schools in that city, he attended the University of Maryland where in 1954 he received his B.A. Three years later he was awarded an M.A. at Indiana University Following three years as an instructor of English at the University of North Dakota, he returned to the University of Maryland where, in 1965, he was granted a Ph.D. Since then he has been with the English Department at Murray State University in Murray, Kentucky. Recently, he has published several articles on F. Scott Fitzgerald as well as essays on Nathaniel Hawthorne, Theodore Dreiser, and Willa Cather.

Preface

Best known for the novels he wrote with Charles Nordhoff, James Norman Hall was in his own right a prolific and distinctive author. More reflective and more varied in his interests than Nordhoff was, he injected many of his values and even personal experiences into the works he wrote with his collaborator. But his ideas emerge most compellingly in selections he produced without a partner, particularly in his collections of essays and sketches: *On the Stream of Travel, Mid-Pacific, Under a Thatched Roof,* and *The Forgotten One and Other True Tales of the South Seas.*

One must not assume that Hall limited himself to writing about the South Pacific. Although he resided in Tahiti for three decades, his attention ranged over the globe and across centuries. Polynesia, to be sure, was his haven from the commercialism and technology he believed to be ravaging the modern world. But his writings abound in reminiscences about and criticisms of his native America and of Europe where he had served in World War I first with the British Infantry and later as an aviator with the Escadrille Lafayette.

His turning to Polynesia, however, was not a rejection of his American heritage. In the South Seas he sought the features of his boyhood home in Colfax, Iowa, that he most treasured—serenity, smallness of scale, slowness of change, and a closeness to nature. His principal complaint against industry and commerce was that, in their cancerous growth after the First World War, they were destroying the most valuable qualities of villages like Colfax throughout the United States.

Hall's timeliness (and perhaps timelessness) lies in his refusal to concede that the things he valued were irrevocably lost. He believed that in even the worst of times they could be preserved in an individual here and an isolated community there and that such preservation gave hope for the regeneration of a world defiled by greed and violence. It would be too glib to proclaim him a precursor of the ecology movement or of the pacifism and the communes of the late 1960s and 1970s. He disliked fads and no doubt would have been amused by the silliness and offended by the excesses which have characterized these phenomena. Yet, more than most of his contemporaries, Hall was appalled by the forces which have distressed so many people recently. And the world he yearned for would appeal to more sensitive, informed persons of the present than would the worlds sought by Pound, Eliot, Lawrence, Hemingway, Faulkner, or Céline—a random but representative list of writers prominent when Hall was producing his best work.

True, like many authors of his time, Hall expatriated himself. And he shared the tendency that Edmund Wilson noted of writers in the 1920s to take refuge from the "perplexities and oppressions" about them by "retreating into a fantasy land" which was usually an idealization of a bygone era or of a contemporary region remote from the centers of power.[1] But Hall's Polynesia and his turn-of-the-century rural Iowa, unlike Lawrence's Mexico, Eliot's pious old England, Pound's Provence and Italy, Yeats's Byzantium, and Hemingway's Africa and bull ring—violent or authoritarian places all—were peacefulness and brotherhood epitomized. Both places came to represent for him values he held to be essential for the psychic well-being of mankind. Those values served Hall himself well. Not merely did he retain his sanity in a world he perceived as going mad, but he also preserved his sense of humor, his pleasant disposition, and, except for a period in the wake of the Second World War, his optimism.

Few of us, of course, read an author simply because he expresses timely sentiments or even provocative ones. We demand that he write persuasively, distinctively, or entertainingly. The last of these Hall could nearly always do whether working with or without Nordhoff—hence his popularity. Hall's problem from the standpoint of his reputation among scholars and serious critics has been that his most widely known works, the Nordhoff and Hall romances, are the ones most likely to be dismissed as mere entertainment. True, these books are often melodramatic. But even the less successful among them are not devoid of subtleties and ambiguities, some of which inevitably grew out of the interplay between the temperaments and attitudes of the two authors. I shall examine, therefore, all twelve of these volumes, giving more attention, of course, to the *Bounty* trilogy and *The Hurricane* than to lesser efforts such as *The Dark River* and *The High Barbaree*. In these portions of my study, although I do not ignore Nordhoff's contributions, I emphasize how these works embody Hall's attitudes.

All sixteen volumes which Hall produced without his literary Siamese twin are discussed.[2] The largest proportion of space is allotted to his essays and sketches, in part because it is impossible to cover adequately several dozen self-contained short works in a few paragraphs, but also because it is in these selections that the ideas and personality of Hall emerge most strikingly. In my final chapter I consider possible reasons why these writings have received less critical attention than I believe they deserve.

As for Hall's poetry, it has neither received much critical comment nor, from a strictly aesthetic standpoint, does it deserve much. No one is likely to reject the judgment of Hall's friend and editor, Ellery Sedgwick, that most of these poems are pleasant in an old-fashioned way but are lacking in distinction.[3] But, distinctive or not, *The Friends, Oh Millersville!* and *A Word for His Sponsor* illuminate facets of Hall's thought and character germane to this study—hence the space I give them. For similar reasons I devote more than a few paragraphs to his two novels: *Lost Island*, a small thing done well, and *The Far Lands*, a big thing done less well. His eighteenth-century-framework tale, *Doctor Dogbody's Leg;* his three war books; his book-length account of his visit to Pitcairn Island; and his autobiography are all at least interesting, and some are more than that. Thus, they are entitled to the pages I give them in this study.

Having dutifully read all four dozen-plus of Hall's magazine offerings, I can confidently assert that nearly all the best of them found their way into Hall's books. There they appear, to be sure, with minor revisions and often under new titles. But the changes are generally too slight to warrant discussion. The periodical pieces which Hall did not resuscitate in one of his books are mainly either very minor poems or equally minor travel articles or vignettes. There are, however, a few exceptions, and these I comment upon in my text.

Acknowledgments

I wish to express my gratitude to Little, Brown and Company and to Houghton Mifflin Company for permission to quote from copyrighted material by James Norman Hall.

I must thank Professor Lynn Bridwell and the other members of the Murray State University Committee on Institutional Studies and Research and Mr. Billy J. Puckett and the M.S.U. Foundation for providing financial assistance to enable me to do research on Hall. Ms. Betty Hornsby of the M.S.U. Library was enormously helpful to me, as was Ms. Anne G. Kintner of the Grinnell College Library and Mr. Bernard A. Bernier, Jr., Head of the Reference Section of the Serial Division of the Library of Congress in Washington, D.C. Gratitude is also in order for Professor Leonard Lutwak of the University of Maryland, who directed my doctoral dissertation from which portions of this study were derived.

To Dr. Sylvia E. Bowman, editor of TUSAS, I am grateful. I must also thank Ms. Alberta M. Hines of TUSAS for her helpful advice. The typing of Leesha Hazel and the editorial assistance of Suzanne Hill, of my daughter, Kathy, and especially of my wife, Helen, have been indispensable.

Chronology

Nordhoff and Hall's adventures in Polynesia. The two men settled in Tahiti but pursued separate careers.

1922   Hall returned to the United States, stopping off at the Marquesas Islands. Went to Iceland. Unable to complete book about it.

1923   Had difficulty in Tahiti disciplining himself. Nordhoff's career was flourishing.

1925   Hall, aged thirty-seven, married sixteen-year-old, part-Polynesian Sarah Winchester. The marriage was a great success.

1926   *On the Stream of Travel* published. Son, Conrad Lafcadio, born.

1928   *Mid-Pacific* published.

1929   Partnership with Nordhoff resumed with publication of *Falcons of France*, a novel about the Lafayette Flying Corps.

1930   Daughter, Nancy, born.

1932   *Mutiny on the Bounty* published; was a huge success critically and commercially.

1934   Two *Bounty* sequels appear, *Men Against the Sea* and *Pitcairn's Island*.

1936   *The Hurricane* published. Hall and his son both became ill; went to the United States for medical treatment. Nordhoff's marriage collapsed.

1938   *The Dark River* published. Nordhoff's health so bad he could not work. Hall returned to Tahiti.

1939   *The Friends*, a book-length poem, published.

1940   *Oh Millersville!*, a literary hoax, and *Doctor Dogbody's Leg*, a group of extravagant tales set in the late eighteenth century, were published as was *No More Gas* by Nordhoff and Hall.

1941   *Botany Bay* by Nordhoff and Hall published.

1942   Published *Under a Thatched Roof*, a volume of short works, and *Men Without Country*, which bore Nordhoff's name but was mostly Hall's work. Nordhoff settled in California.

1944   *Lost Island*, Hall's novel about the impact of the war on a Polynesian island, published.

1947   On April 11 Nordhoff died of a heart attack. Hall, who was in California for his daughter's wedding, attended the funeral.

1949   *A Word for His Sponsor,* a book-length satirical poem about the threat of nuclear holocaust, published. In November he visited his daughter and her husband in Hawaii. There, with the encouragement of the renowned anthropologist Sir Peter Buck, of the Bishop Museum, he completed *The Far Lands,* a novel set in the dawn of Polynesian history.

1950   *The Far Lands* published. Returned to Iowa for the fortieth reunion of his class at Grinnell: received an honorary degree; suffered paralysis in his leg; and learned in Boston that he was suffering from a serious coronary ailment.

1951   Died at his home in Arué, Tahiti, of coronary failure on July 6. Many mourners attended his funeral. Recording of the Largo from Dvořák's *New World Symphony* played. Interred at a site near his house overlooking Matavai Bay, where the *Bounty* had dropped anchor. A poem he had written as a boy in Iowa was inscribed on his gravestone.

1952   Three works published posthumously: a volume of commemorative verses written for his daughter's birthdays (printed in a private limited edition); *The Forgotten One and Other True Tales of the South Seas,* a collection of six short works, four of which had appeared in earlier volumes; and *My Island Home,* his unfinished autobiography.

CHAPTER 1

Prairie Eden

IN 1920 dissatisfaction with American provincialism was in fashion. H. L. Mencken had been berating it in editorials in *Smart Set,* and Sinclair Lewis had just satirized it in *Main Street.* In *Winesburg, Ohio,* Sherwood Anderson had recently depicted it as a force which warped the lives of sensitive residents of small Midwestern towns. And scores of authors had fled or were shortly to flee to Europe to escape from it—among them T. S. Eliot, Ezra Pound, Gertrude Stein, E. E. Cummings, Ernest Hemingway, and F. Scott Fitzgerald. One might assume, therefore, that when a young writer from Colfax, Iowa, set sail from the United States that year he was rejecting the values of his native milieu.

But James Norman Hall, a man who scorned fashions, was fleeing not what Colfax represented but those trends in modern life which he believed were destroying the Colfaxes of the Western World. In work after work he was to extol the Iowa of his youth. And long after he had settled in Tahiti, he asserted: "All my roots are still . . . in the prairie country of the Middle West."[1] And, instead of denouncing American backwoods Philistinism, he would complain: "Remote villages and rural communities have lost their identity, and their charm and peace have been sacrificed to that worst of abominations, the automobile."[2]

I *The Landlocked Island*

Remote and rural Colfax indubitably was when Hall was born there on April 22, 1887. With a population of 1,794, it was a tiny dot on a map amid a scattering of dots in the main equally small. If life, as Hall was to contend, "must be kept on a human scale" to be interesting and valuable, then existence there should have been a cornucopia of delights.[3]

Hall's own life in Colfax, as he depicts it in numerous

autobiographical writings, seems to have been not unlike the lives
of boys in Mark Twain's Hannibal. There was a similar succession
of picnics, pranks, woodland strolls, and excursions. In Colfax, too,
the twin beams of the community were the family and the Protestant churches. And, like Twain's village on the Mississippi, Colfax
had a social structure that paradoxically was both cohesive and insubstantial. The smallness, homogeneity, and isolation made for
compactness. And in families such as his—where there were
numerous children (five in the case of his own) and often aunts, un-
cles, and cousins nearby—a sense of belonging must have come
easily.

But if Colfax's size made for cohesiveness, its newness could
cause a sense of rootlessness in someone as sensitive as Hall. His distant kinsman, Robert Leland Johnson, has noted that Hall regretted
knowing so little about his ancestry. Such ignorance is hardly
astonishing. The region was not many years removed from its frontier phase. And Hall's father, Arthur Wright Hall, had moved
westward from Louisa County, Iowa, on the Mississippi River a
mere four years before James's birth.[4]

Arthur Hall soon set up a general store in Colfax with his brother
and later became a partner in a company that bottled and shipped
local mineral water. Yet, he was no prairie tycoon. Colfax may not
have been an egalitarian Utopia, but James Norman Hall reports in
his autobiography that there were no extremes of wealth and poverty among the town's residents. He recalls only two houses with
bathrooms, and his own was not one of them. He also says that his
home lacked "comforts and conveniences" and that his mother had
to do nearly all the housework herself.[5]

Throughout his youth Hall worked at part-time or temporary
jobs. During his last two years in high school, he progressed from
handyman to clerk at a dry-goods store managed by John and Billy
Davis, who helped instill in him a lifelong enthusiasm for music.
And in the storeroom of a notions shop where he worked as a
delivery boy, he would pore over books by writers as disparate as
Bryant, Twain, Whittier, and one Will Carleton. It was there on a
"grey winter's day" that, in the pages of Herman Melville's *Typee*,
he first became aware of "the world of the islands"—a world that
would later become his home for more than thirty years.[6]

Colfax may have been, at least in retrospect, a haven for Hall and
a prototype for the refuge he was later to find in the South Seas. Yet
his boyhood in Iowa bequeathed to him a wanderlust that would

often impel him to leave a sanctuary, even his beloved home overlooking Matavai Bay in Tahiti. Then off he would set in search of novel experiences and impressions in places as far-flung as Iceland and the Tuamotu Archipelago. This lifelong impulse to visit new scenes he perceived not as a rejection of wherever he happened to be residing but as part of a healthy process of spiritual renewal. Happiness, he believed, was not "to be had for long if it depended on merely husbanding it in one spot."[7]

The genesis of Hall's urge to roam was doubtless a normal childish curiosity about unfamiliar places reinforced by Colfax's isolation. "In those horse and buggy days," he was to declare, "a town of thirty or forty miles distant was unknown territory to most small boys, with the romantic appeal distance lends it" (230). Most roads were hardly more than rough paths. The only river, the Skunk, was unnavigable. But what the Mississippi was to Sam Clemens or what a copra schooner is to a restless boy on a remote Pacific atoll, the Chicago, Rock Island, and Pacific Railroad was to Hall. Its whistles broke the monotonous silence, and its freight cars brought colorful vagabonds who would tell avid young listeners fascinating tales about locales far away. The cowcatcher of a locomotive would provide the exhilaration of forbidden, dangerous adventure when Hall and a pair of his friends would slip from bed at night, ride to Grinnell thirty-two miles to the east, and return before dawn on a westbound train. It is no wonder, therefore, that to the end of his life, Hall exempted trains from his verbal onslaughts against technology.

But these nocturnal excursions were more than adventures. They were a less bitter prairie equivalent of the fruit of Eden's forbidden tree. What Hall acquired from them, however, was not a knowledge of good and evil but a perception of Colfax's insufficiencies. In the college town to the east he saw buildings that seemed "august and venerable" compared to structures in Colfax. Other dissatisfactions emerged. He does not specify when he first realized that the furniture in his home was "all in atrocious taste" (4). But, as his powers of discrimination developed, his awareness that he was not ensconced in a bower of beautiful artifacts must have grown. Also, many of the verses he was to attribute to a little prairie girl, Fern Gravel, in his literary hoax, *Oh Millersville!*, indicate that he was by no means impervious to the narrowness and violence which could mar village life. And sometimes, like Fern, he must have found the serenity of the prairie palling, especially during the interminable Iowa winters.

If trains provided an intermittent escape, literature afforded an ever-available one. From earliest childhood, when he had listened to his mother read Dickens and Cooper aloud, he was a book addict. Even before he could read he would revel in the illustrations in his father's copies of *Paradise Lost* and *The Rime of the Ancient Mariner*. And in grammar school the compulsory memorization of sentimental verses did nothing to diminish his fondness for poetry. Indeed, throughout his boyhood he was a self-styled woodshed poet. Eventually not only the walls of the family woodshed but of the barn as well were adorned with his fledgling verses.

II   *Campus Idyll*

With high school behind him as well as the ordeal of delivering a commencement oration, Hall was forced to make a decision. H. G. Gould, owner of the clothing store where he worked as a salesclerk, offered him the management of a shop he had recently acquired in Belle Forche, South Dakota. Not yet eighteen, Hall was at first dumbfounded by the opportunity. But he was reluctant to settle down. Then, too, he aspired to become a writer, although thus far his only reward had been a stack of rejection slips.

But Hall did not emulate Ishmael by going to sea. Instead he went to college. He chose Grinnell not so much because it was near-by as because on one of his night trips he had heard the glee club singing a marching song that was to give him "an ideal conception of comradeship" which he claims never to have lost (31).

Back in those benighted days before a bachelor's degree was regarded as an inalienable right of every American able to scribble his name, higher education was something not only to be treasured but, in the case of a far-from-wealthy boy like Hall, to be earned. First he worked as a potato-peeler at a restaurant. Later he was a student waiter at a local hotel which, he soon discovered, turned into a bawdy house at night. One traveling salesman, however, brought something other than concupiscence to the dining room. Curtis W. Coe, a representative of a Congregational publishing house in Boston, wanted to tip Hall. Upon learning that tips were not permitted, he left behind a volume of verse by Francis Thompson, who was to become one of Hall's favorite poets. As for Coe himself, Hall was later to meet him in Boston, and the two remained friends until Coe's death.

Hall, in fact, despite his shyness and his lifelong yearning for solitude, had an extraordinary talent for acquiring and retaining friends. That talent manifested itself no less fruitfully at Grinnell than it was later to manifest itself in Boston, Europe, and the South Seas. The professors also seemed to have liked him, and some took a close personal interest in him. The two who probably had the greatest impact upon him were George B. Pierce and Charles E. Payne. Pierce, head of the school of music, helped to deepen Hall's love of music (although he did nothing to mitigate the conservatism of Hall's preferences). Payne, a history instructor who had lost both legs in a train accident and who walked with artificial limbs, contributed to the development of Hall's literary tastes. Rather incongruously and quite unwittingly, Payne strengthened Hall's urge to go to the South Seas. Certain ambivalent remarks of his about Matthew Arnold induced Hall to read all of Arnold's poems. Most made a negative impression. However, a passage from "Rugby Chapel"—". . . the moonlit solitudes mild / Of the midmost ocean"—had the incredible effect of intensifying his desire to travel to the Pacific (60).

III   *Urban Inferno*

But Hall's ultimate Paradise, like Dante's, was not to be reached without a long preparatory journey. In Hall's case the first circle of hell was Chicago, which he disliked as soon as he caught sight of its "appalling suburbs" (65). The circumstances of his visit hardly predisposed him in the city's favor. Having failed trigonometry in his sophomore year, he needed to repeat the course in order to graduate on schedule. Unfortunately Grinnell offered no summer classes in trigonometry. But the University of Chicago did, so off he set in 1908 for his first encounter with what was to become his *bête noire*, the modern metropolis. Surely nothing thus far could have prepared him adequately for Chicago. In fact, except for trips to nearby Des Moines and some brief exposures to Saint Louis, both much smaller cities than Chicago, he had passed his entire life in little Midwestern towns.

Some young people from the provinces find great urban centers exhilarating and liberating. Hall reacted with almost total revulsion. Indeed, virtually everything about Chicago—its size, its crowdedness, its dirt, its rapid pace of life—was out of tune with his temperament. Instead of being stimulated by the unremitting activity he saw around him, he was depressed by the sight of "millions of people engaged in useless, joyless occupations."[8] And the campus of the university was no refuge during what he was to term a "period of profound disillusionment" (65). On the contrary, it was a microcosm of the surrounding community—large, crowded, and impersonal. Ironically, in Chicago, Hall, who as man and boy loved solitude, was oppressed by loneliness in a new and for him painful form—"the solitude of multitude" (65).

Looking back on his nightmare there, he was to conclude that his most educational experience in Chicago had been his discovery of its slums. Instead of shunning those putrid sores of modern urban life, he deliberately sought them out. Because Hall was anything but morbid, we must accept his explanation that he was atoning for his "ignorance of such places by viewing them week after week so that the romanticist might never forget this side of life in modern Camelot" (66).

IV   Boston and First Publications

And forget he never did. His initial response to these horrors seems to have been an attempt at countering them with more pleasant scenes. After a cleansing year at Grinnell, he set forth in the summer of 1909 to visit a farm in Scotland where Robert Burns had once lived. In the British Isles he bicycled around Scotland and in London saw up close for the first time the machine that was soon to make such a decisive impact upon his life—the airplane. The particular one he viewed had made the first flight across the English Channel on July 25 of that year, piloted by Louis Blériot, and was on display in a department store.

His final year at college passed on the whole agreeably. Then, in 1910, with Halley's Comet to light him on his way, he was graduated from Grinnell. The destination he had chosen was, incredibly, Boston. During commencement week a Grinnell alumnus, C. C. Carstens, director of the Massachusetts Society for the Prevention of Cruelty to Children, had offered him a job as a social worker. Prodded by memories of what he had seen two summers before in the slums of Chicago and of similar sights the following year in Glasgow and London, he accepted promptly. Although he was later to find the role of South Seas lotus-eater congenial, Hall always had a compassion for suffering humanity. He also had a strong sense of responsibility and a disinclination to shun a challenge. Thus the qualities that would lead him to enlist so precipitously first in the British infantry and then in the French air force were leading him back to the urban life he had found so detestable.

Boston, to be sure, was no Chicago. And, for all his bias against cities, Hall was not unresponsive to its charms. He found Louisburg Square, where he rented lodgings, pleasant. Moreover, he enjoyed excursions into the surrounding country, especially to Walden Pond with its resonances of Thoreau, who was understandably one of Hall's favorite authors.

Under the spell of Walden Pond, he extended his acquaintance with Thoreau's writings. In the process, as he grew to admire even more the wholeness of Thoreau's character, he became convinced that his own lacked cohesion. In fact, he was undergoing during his four years in Boston what today might be called an identity crisis. (The phrase, though, would have made the good-natured, straightforward Hall either wince or laugh.) Inseparable from his efforts at self-definition were his struggles to become a successful writer. As before in Colfax, his labors brought him a large collection of rejection slips. When *Century* magazine accepted one of his poems, "Fifth Avenue in Fog," for which it paid fifteen dollars, Hall, sanguine as usual, envisioned money pouring in weekly. Alas, his earnings from publication during those four years totalled twenty dollars, the other five coming from a poem in *The Bellman* entitled "Charwoman."[9]

The poems themselves, like most of Hall's verse, are agreeable but a bit old-fashioned even by the standards of 1914. Agreeable or not, both express his misgivings about cities. In "Charwoman," an Italian sonnet, he contrasts the luxurious lives of the urban rich with the drudgery endured by the poor who serve them. "Fifth Avenue in Fog" is a much more complex work. Its twenty-six lines give a vivid impression of Hall's archvillain among cities, New York, transformed by "the magic of mist" into a lovely vision. Here too is one of the earliest expressions of Hall's belief in not only the power of imagination to elevate a "ponderous, leaden world" but in the ultimate reality of what the imagination perceives. "True is the fine illusion, true!" he exclaimed in 1914 as he was to exclaim again, in effect, in 1950 in his last novel, *The Far Lands*.

But, if such fine illusions had their truth, they could not efface the sterner truths Hall saw daily in the slums of Boston. His work with the MSPCC brought him into constant contact with the most sordid aspects of city life—prostitution, alcoholism, child abuse, and living conditions of unbelievable squalor. Some of his reactions were predictable, as was the empathy which he established with many of the poverty-stricken people he encountered in his casework. Of course, among the poor he saw and was repelled by instances of meanness. Yet he liked many of the people he met, and, without sentimentalizing them, recognized their virtues as well as their vices.

Another young man might have been nudged toward socialism by such experiences. Hall was deterred, however, by the very qualities in his character and background which made him find the city itself so antipathetic—his individualism and his hatred of bigness. He was neither naive enough nor blind enough to accept the contention of a janitor that slum dwellers were happy with their lot. But Hall's own observations compelled him to agree with the man's assertion that children fared better in the most wretched homes than in even well-run institutions. Thus, even this early in his development he was evincing that preference for the small over the large, the informal over the structured, and the personal over the institutional which would later lead him to define himself as an anarchist.

V   *Home Again*

The disharmony between his work and his inclinations may have caused the desperation he came to feel in the winter of 1914-15. No doubt his lack of rapport with Mr. Carstens, the director of the MSPCC, was also a factor. Furthermore, his persistent failure to attract much attention with his writings could hardly have elated him. Dissatisfaction conspired with an opportunity for a new life to make him resign his job in early April. The opportunity was an offer from his old friend and classmate, Chester Davis, to join him in a sheepherding venture in Montana.

It was inevitable that Hall would stop over in Iowa, which he had not visited in four years. At Colfax he realized for perhaps the first time that even his beloved hometown was no longer safe from the scourges of modern technology. Now there was a garage, and he overheard farmers talking about a need for better roads. And just outside of Colfax he was horrified to encounter a sign proclaiming: SEVEN THOUSAND MORE SINCE YESTERDAY—FORD.

Professor Payne, his old mentor, was no less horrified when he learned of Hall's intention of becoming a sheepherder. Payne implored his young friend to become an instructor of English and to shun enticements to which his romantic disposition predisposed him. The danger he singled out for special emphasis was Hall's wanderlust.

CHAPTER 2

The Terrible Purgatory

H ALL never became a Montana sheepherder. The upshot of
Payne's advice to shun the life of "an irresponsible hobo" and
to settle down to a career of teaching, however, was that Hall sailed
for Liverpool on May 27, 1914. "My sudden decision," he ex-
plained, "was prompted by the fear that I might yield to Professor
Payne's plea to enter the teaching profession" (128). Although in
his autobiography Hall may have exaggerated his determination not
to enter the academic world (Paul L. Briand, Jr., points out that he
applied to Harvard to work toward advanced degrees in English),[1]
there is little reason to doubt that he sensed that the sedentary life
of a college professor would have been as uncongenial to him as
social work had been. Then, too, his shyness made public speaking
such an ordeal for him that to the end of his life he shunned it
whenever possible.

In London Hall rented a fourth-floor room in a lodginghouse at
45 Bernard Street W.C. 2. There, for six weeks, he wrote. But when
his labors won him the same reward he had generally received in
America—rejections—he purchased a secondhand bicycle and set
off on a tour of the countryside.

His first destination was the home of Joseph Conrad in Kent. One
of the legacies of his Boston sojourn was an enthusiasm for Conrad's
works, which were to have a greater influence upon Hall's mature
writings than were the works of perhaps any other author. The
shyness, though, which had made him so reluctant to become a
teacher kept him from approaching the door of Conrad's house. So
too did that deeply ingrained respect for an artist's privacy which is
the theme of his amusing account of the incident in "A Person from
Porlock."[2]

He next traveled as far north as Chester then headed toward
Wales, reveling all the while in landscapes that seemed as idyllic as
those of rural Iowa. Few idylls, though, could ever have concluded
24

more abruptly. In the Welsh village of Beddelert, he learned from a uniformed man that England had just declared war on Germany. Hall immediately sold his bicycle, took a train to London, and on August 17 enlisted as a private in the Ninth Battalion of the Royal Fuseliers.

I   *The Horror and the Glory*

A man as complex as Hall is apt to have many motives, some of them unfathomable, for any important decision. The two he usually advanced for enlisting in the British infantry in his many writings on the subject are certainly true as far as they go: a yearning for adventure and a love of England. As a self-acknowledged "Romanticist," he was inevitably caught up in the war fever which swept England in 1914. As a member of a generation weary of peace he must have viewed war as the headiest of stimulants. And, however fond he may later have become of South Sea lotus-eating, he was seldom impervious to the lure of excitement. Then, too, his pair of summers in the British Isles as well as a lifetime of doting on English authors had turned him into a confirmed Anglophile. Germany, on the other hand, his affection for some of its composers notwithstanding, had never appealed to him, and its current behavior was doing little to increase his esteem for it. There might have been, however, another motive. It is no discredit to Hall to suggest that, as an aspiring writer, he sensed he had at last found a subject that could inspire him to produce work which would interest others. Be that as it may, the war did provide him with such a subject.

Of course, the rigors of training and the ordeals of trench warfare in France left him no time to produce publishable literature. During his many months as a machine gunner, Hall saw more than his share of dying and had at least his share of encounters with death. But he was also storing up both in his journal and in his brain impressions which he would have an opportunity to utilize far sooner than he could have expected. As the war dragged on through 1915, even an optimist like Hall had to realize that the conflict was likely to be a long one. Prospects for an early end to the fighting seemed especially bleak after the Battle of Loos, a disaster in which more than sixty thousand men were slaughtered to gain one mile of territory along a four-mile front. But an occurrence as melodramatic as anything in the romances he was to write with Nordhoff snatched him from the trenches and whisked him off to safety in the United States. One day he was summoned to battalion headquarters where the adjutant informed him he was to leave the army at once. What had happened was that Hall had written to a friend in Boston asking him to use his influence to secure for him permission to visit his father, who was dying from Parkinson's disease. Instead of a leave, Hall had been granted an honorable discharge.

And so, after a year and ninety-nine days in the infantry, he voyaged back to his homeland "a happier, more miserable man" (159). The cause of his happiness is self-evident. The misery, however, grew out of his feeling that, although the circumstances of his departure were beyond reproach, he was somehow guilty of abandoning his comrades in a crisis. That feeling lingered throughout his stay in America—a stay that was to be short but productive.

Of the many friends Hall acquired throughout his sixty-four years, few were more valuable than Ellery Sedgwick, editor of the *Atlantic*. An item in the *Boston Globe* about Hall had first brought him to Sedgwick's attention. Suspecting that the story of an American fighting with British troops would be of interest, he asked Hall to write a series of articles about his experiences. Sedgwick's motives, however, were not entirely literary. A sympathizer with the Allied cause, he wanted to increase interventionist sentiment in this country. He was shrewd enough, nevertheless, to caution the young veteran against heavy-handed didacticism and to suggest a leavening of humor.

Before starting on the project, Hall returned to Iowa. There he was appalled by the all-but-universal indifference to the carnage in Europe. Despite his fear of public speaking, he gave a lecture about the war in the Methodist church and was aghast when the audience laughed at a grim story he told to demonstrate the hardiness of the British troops. That anguish plus his guilt over abandoning a cause he had come to regard as his own made him want to flee back to France. But his old mentor, Professor Payne, helped convince him that the articles would be a significant contribution to the war effort.

II *First Book*

The articles were collected into a book published later that year (1916) by Houghton Mifflin, then an *Atlantic* affiliate. Entitled

Kitchener's Mob, it is a first-person narrative which recounts Hall's experiences first as a trainee in the British army and then as a machine gunner on the front in France. Episodic and anecdotal, it is often humorous without in any way mitigating the horror of its subject matter.

Although the chapters are fairly self-contained, their cumulative effect is that of an initiation story. The youthful narrator goes off to war almost as a lark. As an American, he inevitably has some difficulty adjusting to English ways. When he tries talking like the British he fails dismally. British class distinctions also trouble him initially. But, without ever becoming entirely comfortable with them, he learns to accept their utility as a means of imposing discipline on raw recruits—a quality in which he feels that democracies in general are woefully deficient.

Although the humor by no means disappears, the tone darkens after the action moves to France, especially after a smiling man to whom Hall has been talking receives a wound which disfigures him horribly. As the war continues, the men learn to respect an enemy who is being ridiculed in the British press. The reality of trench warfare soon leads Hall to a recognition of "the tremendous sadness, the awful futility of war."[3] As the horrors multiply, Hall learns not just that war is ghastly but that beneath British stolidity lies genuine heroism. He also comes to realize that he himself possesses unsuspected reserves of strength. Despite the value of such lessons, he is appalled by the barbarity of "so-called Christian nations." And when an English soldier asserts, "If this 'ere is a sample o' Christianity, I'll take my chances down below," Hall utters not a syllable in protest (191). He does proceed, though, to conclude the work with a paean to the tenacity of the British troops.

Like most of Hall's books, *Kitchener's Mob* was well received. Although Hall was later to speak disparagingly of it, it deserves praise. It is, in the main, a moving, honest account of life in the trenches. Without glamorizing combat, it conveys the sense of adventure soldiers felt during the initial phases of the conflict. Furthermore, for a book written in 1916 by a partisan of the Allied cause, it is astonishingly free of rancor toward the Germans, at least as individuals.

The book, to be sure, has faults. Rather than trust his memory and imagination to provide concrete specifics to convey the mood of his comrades, he sometimes resorted to the clumsy device of using the words and actions of a composite British infantryman with the

generic name of "Tommy Atkins." This device results not merely in
an abstractness which blunts the impact of the work but in an occasional sentimentalizing of the British forces. When he deals with
specifics his eye is clear, his prose controlled. When he regards the
British army collectively, however, his vision wavers, and the words
go soft. Then it becomes good old Tommy this and dear old Tommy
that and sounds unwittingly patronizing.

Another defect grows out of one of Hall's more commendable
qualities—his modesty. Since this is his story as well as the story of
the British army, he should emerge as a more clearly defined figure.
Later, Hall would learn to convert his own character into a useful
persona, a sort of bemused eccentric with common sense and a
fondness for reminiscing and philosophizing. His discursive method
of writing, with its tendency to veer between narration and exposition, requires the controlling center such a persona can provide.
Kitchener's Mob lacks that center.

What it does not lack is the power to engross and affect the
reader. The writing is vigorous and at its best communicates a sense
of what life and death in the trenches were like. Paradoxically the
humor that Sedgwick had urged Hall to inject augments the war's
awesomeness. The facetious remarks of the British soldiers and of
Hall himself come to denote a realization that—for men caught in
the coils of a conflict as vast, relentless, and impersonal as a
prolonged natural disaster—laughter is saner than rage or tears.

III   *Other Writings About England at War*

With the publication of *Kitchener's Mob*, Hall's career as a writer
was finally launched. Between the appearance of his first book and
his second, *High Adventure*, the following year, he published a
number of short works in various popular magazines. Most deal
with the war, and the view that they present of it is essentially the
one expressed in *Kitchener's Mob*. Two, however, merit special
attention because they make points that were to become recurring
themes in Hall's postwar works.

The earlier of the two, "Poetry Under the Fire Test," is a story in
which an old friend, Mason, a veteran of the Battle of Loos, tells the
narrator of how out on the front he encountered a British soldier
reading aloud Milton's "Comus."[4] What emerges from the anecdote is a theme that Hall was never to relinquish—that literature
can help one endure even the most ghastly occurence.

The second work, an article entitled "The Unromantic English," elaborates on a point raised but developed quite differently in *Kitchener's Mob*—that the English are too stolid to realize that they are in the midst of one of history's greatest adventures. A friend from America insists to Hall that the British are incorrigibly unromantic. Unable at the time to rebut the contention, a few days later he thinks of a "brilliant rejoinder": "Romance is realism at a distance. It is nothing more than grim, forbidding reality seen at the end of a vista, either of time or space."[5] Here, near the beginning of his career, is perhaps the most explicit statement of an idea which pervades his work even to the point of governing its shape. Reminiscence and travel, twin constants throughout his essays and fiction, become devices for transforming reality into romance—of distancing events, in other words, so that they could be perceived with the kind of transfiguring glow with which he needed to invest them in order to express them.

CHAPTER 3

The Escadrille Lafayette

IN the two years between the publication of Hall's first and second books, he was to have more adventures than most people experience in their entire lives. The man primarily responsible for those adventures was his editor, Ellery Sedgwick, who had already begun to assume his role as Hall's guardian spirit. Sedgwick asked Hall if he would care to go to France to write some articles on the Escadrille Lafayette, a newly formed squadron of American airmen fighting for France.

Hall eagerly accepted the offer. In Paris he quickly became acquainted not only with several pilots in the Escadrille but with Dr. Edmund Gros, an American who was a director of the American ambulance service and who was closely involved with the new aerial unit. When Hall told Gros of his intention to reenlist in the British army, the latter persuaded him to join instead the French air service.

Perhaps almost as incredible as the combat record Hall was to achieve was the fact that he became a pilot at all.[1] Yet this enemy of machines, who could never bring himself to learn to drive an automobile, became a superb aviator. So skilled were his acrobatics during combat that they dazzled the ace of aces, Eddie Rickenbacker, whose flight commander Hall was briefly.[2] His skill was fully equaled by his daring. Back when aviation was hardly out of its infancy, the mere process of flying was dangerous enough even without the added menace of enemy fire. Engines were constantly dying, objects coming loose, and controls jamming. Furthermore, members of the Escadrille flew without parachutes because the ones then in existence were too bulky for their small pursuit planes. Forced landings were commonplace; and when Hall's war service was abruptly terminated by the crash that put him in a German prisoner of war camp, it was not enemy gunfire but the ripping off of defective wing covering that brought him down.

Before Hall's French-built Nieuport had plunged to the ground on May 7, 1918, he had sent off to Sedgwick eleven chapters of *High Adventure*, a book about his experiences in the Escadrille, now enlarged into the Lafayette Flying Corps. Much of the material had already appeared serially in the *Atlantic*, and the rest was scheduled to be printed there. But, although Hall had been unable to write his two projected concluding chapters, Houghton Mifflin decided to issue the book without them.

I *War in the Sky*

Like his other two World War I Books, *Kitchener's Mob* and *Flying with Chaucer*, *High Adventure* exists in a no-man's land between autobiography and fiction. All three adhere closely enough to facts for portions of them to have been placed, often verbatim, in Hall's posthumously printed autobiography, *My Island Home*. Moreover, like Melville's *Typee* and *Omoo*, they depend for their impact at least in part on the reader's accepting the essential authenticity of what is recorded. At the same time, any discerning person will suspect that, like a novelist or even merely a good raconteur, Hall is heightening, omitting, and rearranging events to maximize their drama.

Perhaps more noteworthy is what he does to himself, because the "Hall" who narrates *High Adventure* is by no means identical with the James Norman Hall of the Escadrille Lafayette. Hall, the Romantic who invests even rather ordinary occurrences with glamour, becomes Drew, a young recruit from Massachusetts. Drew, in fact, is given some of Hall's own most spectacular adventures, including a near-fatal crash after an encounter with a German patrol. It is also Drew, rather than the narrator, who writes the poem Hall had modeled on Alan Seeger's "Rendezvous With Death" and had sent to Curtis Coe, the book salesman who in Grinnell had given him a volume of Francis Thompson's verses. (Coe was to use the poem, "An Airman's Rendezvous," to sell thousands of dollars' worth of Liberty Bonds.)

No doubt the modesty that had prevented Hall from making himself heroic in *Kitchener's Mob* kept him from projecting himself as a dashing figure in *High Adventure*. Since his authorship of "An Airman's Rendezvous" was not a total secret, however, the Drew device may have been partly a joke. If so, the joke is by no means entirely at the unknowing reader's expense because Drew, while heroic, is also something of a fool given to grandiose utterances and to fits of maudlin despondency as well as of exaltation.

The narrator is a different sort of person. Although just as innocent as Drew and equally prone to blunders, he is more restrained, less imaginative, and more inclined to laugh at himself. He also has a common-sense skepticism that, nevertheless, does not make him unresponsive to the romantic visions of his friend any more than Huck Finn's skepticism prevents him from getting caught up in Tom Sawyer's fantasies.

High Adventure thus becomes the comments of the unheroic, rational side of Hall upon his less rational, demonic side. The use of an analytical alter ego to deal with the behavior of a character about whom the author has ambivalent feelings may have been suggested to Hall by his idol Joseph Conrad's use of Marlow in *Lord Jim* and *Heart of Darkness* to explain the ambiguities of Jim and Kurtz respectively.

It would be difficult, however, to find a book less Conradian in design, style, tone, or texture. *High Adventure* has none of Conrad's groping quality. The narration is straightforward, lucid, even abrupt. Furthermore, there is none of Conrad's somber foreboding. The tone throughout is almost breezy. Seldom is there that sense of laughing in order not to cry that often appears in *Kitchener's Mob*. Clearly, flying did exhilarate Hall as it exhilarates Drew and the narrator of *High Adventure*. And even though he does not allow that exhilaration to obliterate his awareness of the horrors of war, he never abandons his view of aerial combat in those marvelous rickety new toys as a thrilling game, albeit for extremely high stakes. It is surely significant that it is the romantic Drew, not the more common-sense narrator, who learns what Hall, the former infantryman, hardly needed to be taught: that from the ground fighter's standpoint war has no glamour—"that it has long since become a deadly monotony, an endless repetition of the same kinds of horror."[3] Both men come to believe, moreover, that "if wars can be won only by haphazard night bombardment where there are women and children, then they had better be lost" (184).

But Drew and his companion can take comfort from reflecting that as pursuit pilots they do not have to bomb civilians. Danger, they may face daily. And many of their comrades are killed. But death usually comes with a merciful swiftness too often denied to men in the infantry. And, unlike men trapped in the trenches, they live comfortably between their brief sorties, eating well-prepared food and sleeping in warm, dry beds.

Although the book is unfinished, the last chapter Hall wrote before his capture by the Germans makes an effective conclusion. In it a visiting American dignitary gives the embarrassed pilots a pompous speech—a fittingly low-keyed ending that does nothing to dispel the mood of the preceding pages.

In most respects *High Adventure* is more effective than *Kitchener's Mob*. For one thing, Hall is patently more comfortable with its subject matter. In his first book he had dealt with events about which he had had unresolved emotions—a disgust at trench warfare, affection for his British comrades, a sense of guilt over having left the army before the end of the war, irritation over the incompetence of the high command, and support for the British cause. Great novelists at the peak of their imaginative powers can sometimes overcome such difficulties. But the matter-of-fact, quasi-journalistic approach Hall had used in his first book could at best gloss them over. In *High Adventure*, however, Hall had no such problem. He loved flying, had developed a zest for aerial combat, admired his comrades in the Escadrille, and had every reason to be proud of his own record with them. He could tell his tales, consequently, with an unrestrained gusto well suited both to his sanguine temperament and to his no-nonsense colloquial style. The narrative, moreover, is better focused than in the earlier book because the narrator is more clearly defined.

Yet the use of Drew as the narrator's more heroic alter ego suggests that Hall was still having persona trouble. Drew may often be a valuable distancing device between Hall and some of his own exploits and emotions. But he is a device that the author at times seems to find unwieldy. Whenever Drew disappears, the narrator often thinks and even behaves disconcertingly like him. Furthermore, we get the impression that Drew sometimes reappears simply because Hall felt that, having introduced him, he could not allow him to vanish.

By and large, though, throughout *High Adventure* Hall speaks with the voice which was to characterize his work thereafter except when he merged his literary identity with Nordhoff's. It is the engaging voice of a man who is reliable and good-natured, wholesome and modest. He is also a man who is humorous enough to tell a joke at his own expense but proud enough not to play the buffoon. All that is missing is the more romantic part of Hall, which he has assigned to Drew. Later, with the war and its opportunity for prodigious heroism behind him, Hall could record his newer experiences without fear of sounding boastful. Drew could then be absorbed into James Norman Hall, traveler, author, lotus-eater.

II *Enter Nordhoff*

Hall's experiences as a German prisoner of war may have been less spectacular than his adventures as an aviator, but they are no less interesting. An account of them, however, must wait until the discussion of his book on the subject, *Flying With Chaucer*, which was not to appear until 1930.

Back in France, following a solitary farewell flight over the front, he met the man to whose name his own would become almost unbreakably welded—Charles Bernard Nordhoff. The two men were brought together by Dr. Edmund Gros, who wanted them to collaborate on a history of the Lafayette Flying Corps and of its nucleus, the Escadrille Lafayette. Few friendships could ever have begun less auspiciously. Hall was later to confess in *My Island Home* that his first impression of his partner-to-be was quite unfavorable (229). Nordhoff, in fact, struck him as being stiff, overbearing, and cold. This negative impression was hardly altered for the better when Nordhoff proceeded to complain about the Iowans who were overrunning his native California.

In view of the dissimilarities between the two men, the prolonged friendship soon to develop between them is more surprising than their initial coolness toward each other. Hall, as we have seen, had been brought up in semirural Iowa in, at best, moderately comfortable circumstances. After working his way through a small prairie college, he had been a social worker in the slums of Boston and had been a prisoner of war. Nordhoff, on the other hand, was the son of wealthy parents and bore the name of a grandfather who had been a well-known traveler, adventurer, and author. He had spent much of his boyhood on the family ranch in Baja California; and, after graduating from Harvard in 1909, he had supervised a sugar plantation in Mexico. Later he and his father opened a clay-processing factory near San Diego. These differences in background were more than matched by differences in tastes, personality, and even of appearance. Hall was dark complexioned and thin to the point of emaciation; Nordhoff was such a gourmet that he was chosen to be mess officer of his predominantly French unit. Hall was casual;

Nordhoff was fastidious. Hall was reflective, even meditative; Nordhoff preferred action. The differences seem endless.

Yet three things were to unite them. Both loved flying. Both were writers. And both yearned to go to the South Seas. Nordhoff had not joined the French flying service until June 1917, nearly a year after Hall's enlistment in the Escadrille Lafayette, having hitherto served as an ambulance driver since the fall of 1916. No less skilled and courageous than Hall, Nordhoff had been mortified by his transfer to a desk job on the executive staff of the United States Air Service in Paris, where he was to remain until the end of the war. Ironically, his writing had put him there. Unlike Hall, who had aspired to authorship since childhood, Nordhoff had become a writer almost by accident. Nordhoff's mother had sent some of his letters from the front to Ellery Sedgwick, who had been impressed enough with them to publish them in the *Atlantic*. When his fame as an author reached the high command, his superiors decided to put his pen to work editing military reports.

III   *America and the Madding Crowd*

After gathering material for their history of the Lafayette Flying Corps in Paris, Nordhoff and Hall returned in February 1919 to America. There they did most of their writing on Martha's Vineyard and completed the history by fall of that year.

About it little need be said here. On the title page Nordhoff and Hall are listed not as authors but as editors, with Edgar Hamilton, who assisted them with the research, designated associate editor. And, in truth, the two-volume work was not "written" by them in the sense that *Mutiny on the Bounty* and *The Hurricane* were to be. Rather it is a huge compilation of facts about the corps, with sketches of and reminiscences by its members. The presentation is resolutely objective. Indispensable to anyone seeking specifics about the corps, it would not have much interest for the general public. In fact, the work was prepared for members of the corps and their friends and relatives. But had not William K. Vanderbilt subsidized printing costs, few could probably have afforded to purchase a copy.

Little that Hall had seen of his native country before sequestering himself on Martha's Vineyard had caused him to abandon his desire to go to the South Pacific. The increased noise, the proliferation of automobiles, and the appearance of other technological horrors

repelled him. Actually Hall seems to have been an early victim of
that phenomenon which Alvin Toffler was to label "future
shock"—a sense of becoming overwhelmed and disoriented by an
ever-accelerating pace of life with novelty following novelty in diz-
zying succession. He was later to assert that change appealed to him
only when it occurred as "slow and cautious advancement and slow
and imperceptible decay."[4]

But, in addition to hating the growing rapidity of life, Hall was
repelled, as was his new friend, by the increasingly strident commercialism. Recalling his stay in America during this period, he was
to write:

The army of Babbitts, as yet unnamed, was then gathering numbers and
impetus and confidence. The leaders were organizing their battalions, and
shouting ecstatic battle-cries from the fortieth floor windows of Chambers
of Commerce. The high priests of the twin-headed god, Business and
Science, were converting people by tens and hundreds of thousands to the
belief that the god was as beneficent as he should be all-powerful, and that
he would make them free and happy beyond their fairest dreams of yesterday. "Produce—Consume!" was gathering currency as a watchword
throughout the land.[5]

It is little wonder the two young men were eager to travel to a
portion of the globe which seemed to epitomize tranquility. But. in
order to get there, they needed money. Off they went to their mentor, Ellery Sedgwick, who told them that the *Atlantic* no longer
published travel articles. Sedgwick, though, referred them to the
editor of *Harper's*, Thomas Wells, who gave them an advance of
seven thousand dollars for a series of articles and a book to be based
on those articles.

Then, while Nordhoff lingered in New York, Hall set off on what
for him with his shyness loomed as a terrifying ordeal—a lecture
tour. He found the experience less ghastly than he had anticipated,
probably because he had memorized his talk. But his observations
throughout the country confirmed his distaste for the tenor of life in
postwar America. One sight particularly repelled him. In California,
where he was to meet Nordhoff, he was so offended by the oil wells
off the Pacific Coast between San Francisco and Los Angeles that
he wrote a sonnet which concluded with the following bitter
couplet:

> They must be vermin, surely, who defile
> Their very Homeland coasts, mile after mile.

In late January 1920 Hall, accompanied by Nordhoff, left those coasts behind as their ship sailed toward Polynesia.

CHAPTER 4

The Happy Isles

WRITERS who dread having their prose tinged with purple should shun Tahiti. Almost everything about the place seems to impel an author to use every word in his vocabulary connoting lushness, beauty, warmth, joy, and charm. And the words, whether moving or embarrassing, evidently express a spell only the most obdurate visitor can resist. Hall not only did not resist the spell but loved Tahiti boundlessly from the moment he first saw it from his ship on a calm, clear February morning in 1920.

No writer, in fact, has ever been more faithful to Tahiti. Others, after making protestations of love, have seldom lingered long. Hall was soon to settle down there and to remain there, except for occasional trips abroad, until his death in 1951.

He made the first such trip not long after his arrival. Hall voyaged on a copra schooner about the Tuamotu Archipelago, a chain of coral atolls to the east, in search of material for the book he and Nordhoff had contracted to write for *Harper's*. Nordhoff, meanwhile, was in the Cook Islands. Although the South Seas was not in 1920 the overworked subject it has since become, Tahiti itself was hardly *terra incognita* for readers. Not only had nineteenth-century authors such as Melville, Charles Warren Stoddard, Stevenson, Henry Adams, and Pierre Loti written about it—in just the previous year W. Somerset Maugham had used it as the setting of *The Moon and Sixpence*. With the Cook and Tuamotu groups as their subjects, Hall and Nordhoff faced no similarly formidable competition. Moreover, the enormous popularity in 1919 of Frederick O'Brien's book about the Marquesas Islands, *White Shadows in the South Seas*, indicated that there was a substantial market for writings about the more remote portions of Polynesia. [1]

I *A Galaxy of Atolls*

Paradoxically, Hall's salient qualities manifested themselves more clearly in his first joint South Sea effort with Nordhoff than they had done in the two books he had written without a collaborator. In *Faery Lands of the South Seas,* the two men made no attempt, as they were to do in the novels they produced later, to blend their talents. Instead, they resorted to a device that Hall admitted was almost the clumsiest they could have employed. Hall in a series of sketches recounted his wanderings through the Tuamotu Archipelago with Nordhoff's accounts of his experiences in the Cook Islands interspersed throughout in the form of letters to Hall. But clumsy or not, the device did not prevent the book from selling well enough to remain in print for ten years, nor did it deter reviewers from praising it. No less an enthusiast of Polynesia than Frederick O'Brien found it a "beautiful and true portrayal of life in the atolls of the Pacific" and commended the authors for writing "in an undertone, carefully, restrainedly, but with an appreciation of the values of romance and the bizarre atmosphere of their activities."[2] The device of the two narrators, moreover, had the further merit of preserving the individuality of the two authors.

Nordhoff's contributions rely more heavily than Hall's do upon narrative and are less discursive. They are also more impersonal. In them, what Nordhoff sees and hears is usually more important than what he thinks and feels. Hall, on the other hand, provides glimpses of his boyhood in Iowa, references to his wartime experiences, and an account of his adventures in Paris after the armistice. A native's song reminds him of a vaudeville team he had once seen back in America; a church dinner on an atoll evokes recollections of a similar dinner back in America. Hall seldom abandons his own point of view. Even when reporting the adventures of someone else, he comments frequently.

Despite Nordhoff's greater narrative flair, Hall's chapters are as absorbing as his partner's. And, as character studies and comments upon life, his accounts of Crichton, the educated Englishman who hides himself on one of the most remote atolls in the Pacific, and the tale of a man who has wasted seven years on another island in a futile search for buried treasure surpass Nordhoff's contributions. One reason for their effectiveness, strangely enough, may be the digressions themselves. T. S. Eliot's observation about Byron could

well apply to Hall: "Digression, indeed, is one of the valuable arts
of the story-teller. The effect of Byron's digressions is to keep us interested in the story-teller himself, and through this interest to interest us more in the story."[3]

An attractive feature of Hall's chapters is that they reveal a
genuine sympathy for suffering men and a feeling for atmosphere.
Despite touches of sentimentality, his accounts of unfortunates like
Crichton and the treasure hunter exude a compassion largely absent
from Nordhoff's chapters. Finally, Hall displays a heartier sense of
humor in *Faery Lands* than does Nordhoff—an ability to laugh not
so much at others as at himself. Thus, when he relates an amusing
incident in which the childlike natives of Rutiaro abandon
themselves to playing with a box of marbles he has brought ashore,
the joke turns out to be on him: the supercargo of Hall's schooner,
angry because the natives' preoccupation with marbles has kept
them from loading the ship, sails off, leaving Hall on the island.

Amid the seeming swirl of incidents and reflections in Hall's portions, moreover, lies a strong, unifying central theme—a repudia-
tion of the demonic will of Western man. His method in each segment is to make his discursive, impressionistic passages coalesce
about some exiled European or American with a self-destructive
goal. In the opening chapter, for example, Hall's apparently random reporting sets the scene for Crichton, who in Chapter II
becomes the focal point of Hall's attention. This kind of development, of course, is reminiscent of Marlow's presentation of Kurtz in
Conrad's *Heart of Darkness*. The Conradian resemblance is
heightened by the fact that Hall, like Marlow, feels both attracted
to and repelled by the object of his curiosity, who eventually
emerges as a sinister alter ego. Crichton's quest, in fact, a yearning
for an isolation so complete that to obtain it he is willing to sequester himself on one of the most inaccessible atolls in the Pacific,
is a mad caricature of Hall's own thirst for solitude which he
proclaims early in the opening chapter.

But whereas Crichton's fanatical reclusiveness leads him virtually
to imprison himself, Hall's "adventure in solitude" is climaxed with
a *fête*. On the atoll of Rutiaro, he decides time has come to act upon
his long-nurtured desire to live completely alone. Off he goes to a
deserted islet nearby. But, lo, the natives soon show up and throw a
splendid feast with entertainment that reminds him of a vaudeville
troop he had seen in Iowa. His experiment shattered, he later
reflects: "If life is to keep its fine zest many wished for experiments

must be perpetually unrealized. . . . Not having been put to the proof, I may still persuade myself that I am a lover of solitude."[4]

The final episode by Hall (Chapters XVI - XVII) concerns someone who even more than Crichton lacks Hall's saving graces, an ability to bend with circumstances and to laugh at himself. The man, an Englishman, has implanted himself on another remote island not to seek solitude but to find gold. Years before, he had bought a treasure map, which is now worthless because it refers to trees no longer in existence. Although he has dug up most of the island, he is determined to remain there until he finds gold. But Hall, who has learned the folly of monomaniacal striving, is convinced the search is futile.

Thus the principal narrative strands bind together Hall's scattered comments about Western commercialism, Polynesian lack of acquisitiveness, the decline of native culture, and the tranquility of the islands into a bundle with which he can slap Western dynamism.

II *An Archipelago of Essays and Sketches*

For the next eight years, in work after work, Hall hymned Polynesia. He praised the cozy smallness of its communities, the beauty of its islands, the amiability of its inhabitants, the slow pace of its life. Although he could confess to having "at moments, a wistful longing for the flesh-pots of New York,"[5] he was nearly always inclined to depict the dearth of Western amenities and amusements as a blessing. Here—without the enticements of motion pictures, radios, and the other appurtenances of modern technology—were people who had not become divorced from the rhythms of nature. Here too were men and women who had not become infected with the Westerner's passion for acquisition and who, consequently, had "ample leisure for everything."[6] Even someone such as himself with a taste for books and conversation above the Jane and Tarzan level could find the tranquility of the South Pacific a boon. "In Tahiti," he insisted, "good talk grows out of ample leisure which gives people time to think of something to talk about . . . and read, something Americans do too little or do too hurriedly, halfheartedly."[7]

Yet these years were not for Hall a period of unremitting bliss. For one thing, he had persistent money troubles. Admiring his semiprimitive neighbors for their lack of commerce was fine. But he was too sensible to commit the supreme folly for a white exile in the South Seas—attempting to "go native." And, even though in "Sing: A Song of Sixpence" he could treat his poverty as a joke which would somehow furnish its own happy ending, there were certainly times when he regarded his financial insecurity as anything but funny.[8]

Having sent most of his earnings from *Faery Lands of the South Seas* to his family, he now depended for his income on his ability to write other marketable works. During much of the early 1920s, however, he was often unable to apply himself. His later editor, Edward Weeks, notes that Hall at this period was seized by "occasional fits of self-doubt and loneliness."[9]

And, in contrast to Nordhoff—who in December of 1920 had married a native girl and who was diligently writing *The Pearl Lagoon*—Hall was plagued by restlessness. After toying with the prospect of returning to France, he fled to Iceland in 1922. Like so many of Hall's actions up to that time, his journey seemed motivated partly by caprice, partly by genuine curiosity, and partly by an urge to find a new subject to write about. He was sufficiently certain that Iceland would inspire him to produce a book to accept for it a five-thousand-dollar advance payment from *Harper's*.

The book was never written. Despite efforts to discipline himself and despite his enthusiasm for Iceland and its inhabitants, he was able to get only a few articles out of his experiences there. Several months later he returned to the United States, gave back the five thousand dollars plus 6 percent interest to *Harper's*, and late in 1923 left Boston for the West Coast, where he would board a ship back to Tahiti.

In the South Pacific he again was unable to work except in spurts. And once more an itch to roam afflicted him, this time to be assuaged by a visit to his friend Arthur Cridland, on an isolated atoll in the Tuamotu Archipelago. The trip, however, was not without profit to him. Cridland had already provided him with material for the opening chapters of *Faery Lands of the South Seas* where, under the name of Crichton, he had been depicted as a bitter recluse. Now, having seen what utter solitude had done to Cridland, Hall wrote an account of his most recent encounter with the man. The result was "The Forgotten One," which was cited in *O'Brien's Best Stories for 1925*.[10]

In 1925, however, an even more important event occurred. Much to the alarm of some of his friends, Hall, aged thirty-seven, married sixteen-year-old Sarah Teravéia Winchester. Sarah, who was one-eighth Polynesian, was the daughter of Joseph Winchester, a sea captain from Liverpool. Once, while sailing with Hall, Winchester had said he would like the younger man to be his son-in-law. When Hall met the girl, he proposed.[11]

But an action that Ellery Sedgwick and others regarded as almost insane proved to be Hall's salvation. Now, faced with responsibility, he began to discipline himself. The birth of a son, Conrad Lafcadio, the following year only increased his feelings of responsibility. An additional inducement to keep writing was a one-hundred-dollar-a-month stipend sent by Sedgwick and the *Atlantic* but, unbeknown to Hall, actually provided by Hall's wealthy friend and fellow resident of Tahiti, Harrison Smith.[12]

In 1926, anybody who, on the basis of having read *Faery Lands of the South Seas,* expected a prolonged, vicarious loll on tropical shores would have been disappointed. Of the fifteen selections in *On the Stream of Travel,* only five deal extensively with Polynesia, and two of these are set principally in Iowa. The rest describe events in places as far-flung as Bavaria and Iceland. But the United States gets the largest share, seven, with four of these devoted to Hall's native state.

Yet most of these selections cannot be pigeonholed geographically. Just as Hall's feet would pace back and forth across the floor when he wrote,[13] so his mind would vault across seas and leap over years. He reminisces, he compares, he philosophizes, and he injects anecdotes. Like the great English essayists whom he admired, he seems a raconteur on paper. Also, like them, he keeps sufficient control of his material to reconcile an informal manner with thematic unity.

The first selection, "A Middle-Western School," sets the pattern for what follows. Nostalgic and elegiac, it celebrates a vanishing village-America and laments its passing. It also presents elements that recur throughout the book—Hall's dislike of "progress"; his attraction to simple people such as tramps, children, and savages; his love of wandering and his kindred recognition of a need to "let go" of things, be they places or obsessions; his retrospective cast of mind; his antipathy toward certain middle-class vices such as self-righteousness, pedantry, and intolerance; and his belief in the power of imagination to revive the past or to transfigure the present.

The work begins with a jocular passage about a school full of

"itinerant professors" in Prairie Hills, the name Hall uses for Colfax
in many of his semiautobiographical writings. The "school" was
held near the railroad yards, and the faculty consisted of vagrants.
There Hall and his youthful friends would listen entranced to
stories about railroad lore and far-off places. He insists that, the
hostility of townspeople toward these men notwithstanding, the
boys learned nothing worse there than "some picturesque
profanity." In fact, he is convinced that "they must have been men
simple of soul and clean of mind" (11). Only one of all he encountered ever took advantage of the boys' gullibility, and he
perpetrated what was a very minor swindle. Some of the men,
moreover, were genuinely gifted. One in particular evoked Hall's
imagination—a virtuoso wood-carver who plied his art on the local
water tower. The work concludes with Hall's returning to Iowa and
searching for the carving. His reward, however, for his "foolish
longing to link past with present days" is the discovery that "the
stockyard school had vanished, and the old water tower had been
replaced by an upright steel pipe which had nothing to commend it
but its utility" (18).

The next selection, "The Azure Lists," would seem to be about as
far removed as possible from its predecessor in subject matter. Yet
this reminiscence about Hall's imprisonment during the war in
Landshut, Bavaria, is also a lament for an irrecoverable past. Here
too, however, memory and imagination struggle with past and present as the captured airmen convert their prison camp into "an
enchanted place" where they recollect the exaltation of flying. But
the joy has become darkened by a realization that the "life of
adventure is at an end" and that "the future can hold nothing to
equal the splendor of the past" (35).

In "Sir John, Miss Amy, Joseph and Charles," Hall seems to be
back in the world of *Faery Lands of the South Seas*. But the
appearance is deceptive. The sketch is less an account of adventures
on his voyage among islands than of an excursion through a realm
he regards as at least as enchanting—the world of literature. The
narrative framework results from his decision to leave his books
behind when he sets off for remote islands because he fears his
reading has become an addiction which has made him too depend-
ent upon the thoughts of other men. But just before Hall departs, a
friend gives him a copy of Froissart's *Chronicles of England*.
Thereafter, throughout his journey he manages to procure from
various people a poem by Amy Lowell; *Lord Jim;* and, in the Mar-

quesas Islands, from a Scotsman with a library "full of trashy adventure stories," a volume of Dickens's *A Christmas Carol.* Here past and present become entwined when Hall spends a part of Christmas day in tropical Typee Valley recalling having heard Dickens's story read aloud on snowy Christmas days in Iowa.

The fourth work, "Sing: A Song of Sixpence," is noteworthy, aside from its value as entertainment, in that it offers a sympathetic treatment of a group of people then much disparaged throughout the islands—the Chinese. Instead of inveighing against their niggardly frugality, their clannish aloofness, and their plodding tenacity as Nordhoff had done in *Faery Lands of the South Seas,* Hall stresses their virtues—their sense of honor, their competence, their family loyalty, and their generosity toward those who befriend them. These qualities are brought to the fore when Hall, failing in his attempt to grow vegetables on his rented property, gives his remaining seeds to a Chinaman, Hop Sing. A short while later Sing has converted them into a garden of marvelous vegetables, many of which he presents to Hall. Thereafter, wherever Hall goes on Tahiti, relatives of the Chinaman heap gifts upon him.

The next selection, in contrast, is one of the grimmest in the collection. Entitled "Onward, Christian Soldiers," it is an exposé of the damage missionaries sometimes do in remote primitive communities. It also offers a pointed, though affectionate, criticism of the moral myopia of pious Midwesterners. On a visit to "Riverview, Iowa," Hall accompanies his aunt to a meeting at church of the Foreign Mission Society. There he is impressed by the earnestness of the principal speaker, a missionary just back from New Guinea. During the talk, when Hall's aunt is called away to minister to a sick neighbor, he accompanies her but leaves her at the neighbor's house and proceeds alone to his aunt's place. Seated on her back porch, he admires the beauty of the Iowa countryside but soon begins thinking about the island of Taputea, where almost the entire population has been killed off. He then recalls a conversation there between a sea captain and a resident naturalist who agreed that much of the blame lay with missionaries, who have destroyed the native folkways and have been harbingers of all the ravages of a predatory alien culture. Hall's own subsequent observations confirm their view, for he finds a society in ruins, giant heathen artifacts desecrated, and a few sickly surviving Polynesians herded into a church to sing "Onward, Christian Soldiers."

Despite the pity and anger pervading this work, Hall depicts the people of Riverview as kindly and sincere. Even the missionary from New Guinea he treats sympathetically. Their sin is not cruelty: it is an ignorance and an ethnocentric pride that merge to abet the demonic will of fanatics. Ironically, the epitaph the story provides for Taputea also could serve as one for many a society in the Western World: "Take from any nation its religion, its secular law, the tradition and immemorial custom which has the all-binding effect of law—what is left? What happens? Precisely what has happened here" (126).

The sixth selection, "Go-Quick Smith," proves that Hall's nostalgia for his boyhood in Iowa did not obliterate his memory of unpleasant occurrences there. Here is a sketch about a brutal farmer who used to torment dogs by putting on their backs a chemical compound called "Go-Quick." One Halloween Smith apprehends Hall in the process of committing a prank, collars him, drags him to the house, and threatens to drown him in a water tank. The terrified boy then faints but is soon revived by a cup of water dashed onto his face by Mrs. Smith. The story ends on a note uncharacteristically harsh: "He may be dead now, and if not, he is a fairly old man, all crippled up with rheumatism, perhaps. If this were the case, it would be no more than he deserves, the old villain!" (154). Thus Hall recognizes that childhood has nightmares as well as dreams.

The next four selections—"Iceland," "From an Hotel Window," "Departure for Spain," and "Snow-Bound"—are products of Hall's ill-fated trip to Iceland. Later he was to protest: "I loved Iceland so deeply that nothing I had written about it seemed worthy of it." [14] Whatever the reason, he seems never to have established the rapport with it that he acquired instantly with Tahiti. Although he admired the Icelanders' dignity and self-reliance, their austere demeanor erected a barrier between them and himself of a kind he had not encountered among the gregarious Polynesians. His frequent impulsive trips and changes of plans, moreover, seem to have had none of the zest they had in the South Pacific. In fact, once he confesses that, while trapped in a chilly room on the northern coast during a snowstorm, he experienced something he never admits to having felt in the South Seas, chronic boredom.

Much of what he extols in Iceland he had already praised about Polynesia and, for that matter, about the rural Iowa of his boyhood—simplicity of life, smallness of scale, closeness of people to nature, and a minimal dependence upon technology. And, much as he had lauded the artistry of Polynesian chants and artifacts, he here praises the Icelandic sagas.

Yet these pages suggest that Hall had difficulty writing about Iceland because, despite his admiration of it, something about it ran counter not merely to his temperament but to his philosophy. For all his own courage in combat and his respect for valor in others, when he took pen in hand the drift of his thoughts was usually toward what A. O. Lovejoy termed "soft primitivism."[15] That is to say his most persistent complaint against modern civilization is not that it breeds indolence, cowardice, or weakness but that it engenders excessive activity, nervous tension, and violence. A "hard primitivist" such as Jack London or Robinson Jeffers might have found Iceland a congenial subject. But those dour Northerners struggling to eke a living from their stark environment were not the true antithesis to those forces Hall most disliked in twentieth-century urban life. Polynesia was.

In "Fifth Avenue in Fog" Hall turns his attention to city life. The title refers to a poem of his published in *Century* magazine in 1914 while he was a social worker in Boston. He begins the selection with a humorous account of how the receipt of fifteen dollars for one of his writings after years of rejections had raised in him the most sanguine expectations. Now he expects similar checks to roll in weekly. In this ebullient mood he begins two new verses but can complete neither. At this point the mood of the work darkens. The setting shifts from his apartment on Louisburg Square to a shabby lunchroom on Dover Street. There he jots down a poem, then heads home, but gets lost in a maze of gloomy streets. Finally he finds himself outside a flophouse and, on impulse, enters and rents a bed for ten cents. After chatting with a vagrant, he scribbles a poem by gaslight as bugs scurry across the wall. He then goes to sleep and remains asleep until awakened at five by the proprietor's bell.

In this work Hall develops two of his favorite themes, the sordidness of urban life and the ameliorative powers of literature, with a gentle self-mockery that in no way reduces the reader's affection or even respect for him. On the contrary, the effect is to make Hall seem not only likable, but self-aware and hence credible.

"And Points West" employs the same elements. In this sketch Hall describes a Christmas spent in an almost-deserted hotel in Chicago. The morning newspaper at his door contains a holiday greeting which only heightens his depression because of its impersonality. Trapped indoors by bad weather, he strolls about the vast building going past indistinguishable doors, floor after floor. Wretched with loneliness, he returns to his room and attempts unsuccessfully to write a jocular article entitled "The Joys of

48   JAMES NORMAN HALL

Wandering." After a solitary dinner, he discovers in the hotel library a copy of *Sailing Around the World Alone*, by Captain Joshua Slocum. Reading the book cheers him up so much that he leaves Chicago that night in good spirits. Here, as in the preceding selection, literature operates as an anodyne. And once again Hall depicts the city as an inhuman monster, in this instance typified by the deserted hotel with its empty corridors and closed doors.

The next offering, "A Desert Town," one of the briefest in *On the Stream of Travel*, can be disposed of quickly. An impressionistic picture of a tiny settlement in the American Southwest, it is most significant as one of the few works in which Hall presents a small, isolated community in unattractive terms. Perhaps his sojourn in Iceland had left him unreceptive toward harsh, treeless environments. Whatever the reason, he clearly found the American desert no rival for Polynesia as a latter-day Eden.

In "The Forgotten One," however, Hall shows how his own paradise can become another man's hell. That man is Crichton, the brooding recluse who, in *Faery Lands of the South Seas*, sequesters himself on the all-but-inaccessible atoll of Tanao. Now, four years later, Hall finds the urge to visit Tanao irresistible. He quickly discovers, however, that living there has brought Crichton anything but contentment. Having neglected to protect his eyes from the intense tropical sunlight, Crichton can no longer read or make sketches to pass the time as he formerly had done. Furthermore, he is now so reclusive that he makes Hall dine alone and indicates through a note that the two probably will not meet again. After sunset, kept awake by the untimely crowing of a rooster, Hall sets off on a stroll around the island. Later he spies Crichton gently stroking the bird and telling it in a calm voice that he has warned it before against such nocturnal noisemaking and that he would now give it a well-deserved punishment. Crichton thereupon rips the living fowl apart. Hall, more appalled by the desperate expression on the bloodstained man's face than by his insane conduct, leaves Tanoa next morning.

Such a bare recital of the narrative's principal incidents cannot convey even a modicum of its horror and poignancy. As in all good storytelling, the effects depend more on tone, pacing, and selection of details than on mere plot. In handling such matters, Hall reveals once more his indebtedness to Joseph Conrad. Again the writing is leisurely and discursive. But, even more than in his earlier account of Crichton, Hall, in "The Forgotten One," makes events converge in a powerful climax.

A major theme, of course, is the perils of extreme solitude. But hardly less important is Hall's admission that even his beloved South Pacific cannot cure a chronically ailing spirit. Small, remote places may be healthier for the robust soul than a frenzied urban milieu is. But the fate of Crichton indicates that a bitter neurotic may be as miserable in the South Seas as in New York. It also suggests that a fanatical pursuit of isolation may be no less dangerous than a monomaniacal pursuit of wealth or progress.

The concluding section of *On the Stream of Travel*, "Why I Live in Tahiti," is more than a paean to the South Seas. It is a statement of Hall's political credo. The setting is Iowa. There his Aunt Harriet startles him by asking him why he lives on "that wretched little island." First he tries to make her understand the appeal of solitude and a simple mode of life. His aunt thereupon raises the question of one's duties, rights, and privileges to which he replies that he is willing to forego his rights and privileges in order to live according to his "own ideas of what constitutes living" (347 - 48). Aghast, she exclaims that he is an anarchist. He agrees she is essentially right because he does long to live someplace where government has been "reduced to the vanishing point." When he tries to clarify his position by explaining that he envisions some kind of Platonic realm rather than an actual state, she refuses to listen.

Now, addressing the reader, Hall says that in Tahiti "one can at least play at anarchy" provided the player has a profession "which provides the necessities of life" (350). Tahiti, also, is not without a government, but it is so far away from the Ministry of Foreign Affairs in Paris that the power of the state is exercised feebly and fitfully. Then too the island can be administered informally because of its smallness. And, since its natives are semiprimitive, their needs can be satisfied without a high level of efficiency or a complex organization. Life there, consequently, is leisurely; dispositions are pleasant; and peace of mind is attainable. Still, he would not urge everyone to come to the island: "The important thing is for the individual to discover for himself the environment best suited to him and stick to it as long as he can. American life in these days is alien to me; it moves too rapidly and there is too little time for the things I love most" (362).

What emerges from all this is not that Hall was an anarchist, as he maintains, but that he was what in today's political parlance would be termed a libertarian. Unlike the Ayn Rands and Milton Friedmans of our time, however, Hall was as hostile to *laissez-faire* economics as to governmental power. As a true conservative who

disliked rapid change and who wished to preserve small traditional
social and cultural units, he recognized that business run rampant
can be as disruptive as the nostrums of a super state. He perceived,
as many self-styled conservatives apparently cannot, that the
business gospel of "Produce-Consume!" can mean only more fac-
tories, more cities and hence more congestion, slums, alienation,
crime, and political turmoil. Thus Hall philosophically had as little
in common with a typical Republican spokesman of either his own
day or ours as he would have had with a Marxist or with a New
Deal-type liberal. Moreover, his compassion for suffering people
would have allowed him little sympathy with the more callous ad-
vocates of *laissez-faire*.

Hall's rejection of politics, in fact, was not so much an evasion of
responsibility as it was a recognition that in the Western world
burgeoning industry had brought about conditions under which the
only viable political movements were for a man like himself equally
intolerable. And so, instead of trying to tolerate the intolerable or to
resist the irresistible, he demonstrated that it was possible for at
least some persons in some places to preserve the ideal of the small,
tranquil, slowly evolving community. In a sense, the old-fashioned
Hall was opting for what in the 1970s would be called an "alternative life-style." He would have eschewed, however, the vulgar
diction and the equally vulgar pattern of thought too often lurking
behind the phrase.

III   *More Essays and Sketches*

Two years later another volume of short works by Hall appeared.
Although its offerings tend to be more genial than those in its
predecessor, *Mid-Pacific* has its rumbles of thunder and flashes of
lightning. The idyllic promise of the title, however, is confirmed by
Hall's preface. There he depicts his home in Tahiti in glimmering
terms and describes himself as lolling under a pandanus tree in-
dulging in reveries and memories which somehow miraculously get
scribbled down on paper. The picture he thus provides of himself
may not accord with that of the real Hall running off to Iceland in
desperation or chain-smoking as he paced across his room trying to
write. But it provides precisely the persona needed by the narrator
of many of the offerings to follow.

The first of these, "Occupation: Journalist," like the opening
chapters of *Faery Lands of the South Seas*, is a purportedly

autobiographical tale in which Hall, sick of the tumult of modern urban life, decides to explore the more remote regions of Polynesia. And, as in the earlier work, the narration soon gravitates toward a white misfit. But the similarities cease there. Crichton, in his obsessive pursuit of solitude, is grand and perhaps tragic. In "Occupation: Journalist," on the other hand, Hall delineates a comic guignol of a human wreck—a swaggering alcoholic ex-sea captain who wants him to edit a manuscript he has written about his life in the South Seas. The old man's work, however, proves to be a tedious account of business transactions devoid of almost anything about island life. When the manuscript disappears, Hall, accused by the captain of stealing it, flees to an uninhabited islet across the lagoon and lives there in blissful solitude until Captain Hardy conveniently dies.

In "Occupation: Journalist," Hall holds up a carnival-house mirror of humor so that what might have been terrifying becomes absurd. The amiable, deftly self-mocking persona Hall maintains, however, prevents his laughter from seeming malicious. In ridiculing Hardy and a punctilious, Tennyson-quoting half-caste administrator, he retains sympathy for the former and affection for the good intentions of the latter. Hall's is the laughter of a man who, recognizing his own foibles, can jest about those of other people like an amused elder brother rather than like a derisive demigod sneering at pygmies.

In "One Kind of Journey" he presents two jokes, both at his own expense. But one of them is not at all funny. He begins with an amusing anecdote about how an urge to leave Tahiti becomes irresistible when, in a Papeete restaurant, he is seized with a longing for buckwheat cakes. The proprietor warns him that trips home are invariably disappointing, but Hall books passage on a tramp steamer to the United States that very day. Back in Iowa, everything at first seems the same. But during an after-dinner walk, he finds his mood darkening as "old ghosts" meet him at every corner. And, when he passes the house of Frank Allbright, who has been paralyzed by a falling tree, he stops to reminisce about how soldiers returning from the Spanish American War once stopped there to pay their respects. Now, many years later, Hall hears the paralyzed man's wife tell a neighbor that Frank is not feeling well and that the hot weather is bothering him. Depressed by what he has heard, Hall concludes that the restaurant proprietor in Tahiti was right about the dangers of returning home.

Like the opening selection in *On the Stream of Travel* ("A Middle-Western School"), "One Kind of Journey" is, of course, an initiation story which makes the point that the past is irrecoverable except within the mind. But there is a major difference. In the work in the earlier collection (both sketches were actually first published in the same year, 1923), Hall depicts a return visit to his hometown that is disillusioning because of the ravages of "progress"—the obliteration of beloved landmarks and the erection of a hideous new metal water tower. But the disillusioning event in "One Kind of Journey" could have occurred anywhere, any time. Trees, after all, can fall on men in tropical paradises as well as in prairie villages and during feudal epochs as well as during the Machine Age. Hall, with all his exposure to misery in the slums of Boston and the trenches of France, did not need to travel thousands of miles from Tahiti to central Iowa to learn that men sometimes suffer unjustly and pointlessly. What he surely intended to suggest is that memory, like imagination, creates its own worlds and that it is unwise to expect those worlds to coincide with the physical realm.

But even though Hall's melancholy conclusion here seems universally applicable, no one should assume that the story shrieks with cosmic despair. The lyricism and the affection for Iowa that dominate the work can no more be effaced by a sad conclusion than a beautiful life can be rendered worthless by a painful, fatal heart attack. Anyone who perceives "One Kind of Journey" as a rejection of either Tahiti or Iowa misunderstands Hall. He is not denigrating his new or his old home; he is exalting the power of the human mind to transfigure events while warning us not to expect what our brains fashion to correspond too closely with what the eye will see and the ear will hear.

Next comes an unfunny story built around a ludicrous situation—an American on a lovely Polynesian island hearing on a radio broadcast from the United States a recipe for sponge cake. As a morally sensitive man who adored the people of the South Pacific, Hall could no more have used death-haunted Nuku Hiva in the Marquesas group to evoke chuckles than he could have made jokes about a World War I cemetery where his comrades were buried. One of the less endearing traits of many radicals of the 1960s was their penchant for glibly mouthing words like "fascist" and "genocide." And of course to equate the unintentional killing off of Nuku Hivans with the deliberate mass murder of Jews by Hitler's henchmen would be to reveal an obtuse lack of moral discrimination. Yet the fact remains that the white man's vices and diseases decimated the once-numerous Marquesan Islanders as thoroughly as the most ruthless policy of willful extermination could have done. Hall, who had first fallen in love with the place after having read as a boy Melville's account of it in *Typee*, was appalled when he contrasted the scenes of desolation before his eyes with the idyllic description of native life in Melville's pages. In "K.F.I.—Los Angeles" he records the experience with appropriate bitterness but also with a dignified restraint that befits what, after all, was more a tragedy than a crime.

"Indian Country" reveals Hall's awareness that he did not need to journey halfway across the world to observe evidence of the destructive power of Western "progress." The sketch recounts a visit to an unnamed Midwestern city which prides itself on its dynamism. Hall, however, feels that it suffers from a "mere rank increase without order of design" as well as from a dreary uniformity (76). One evening on the inside pages of a local newspaper he finds an account of a speech in 1871 by Chief Grey Wolf, who said he did not want to relinquish his tribal lands because the country was like his mother. The author of the article smugly maintains that mere savages could not be permitted to stand in the way of progress. As Hall glances around the hotel lobby filled with vulgar conventioneers, he concludes sadly: "It was hard to imagine that they [the Indians] had ever been within a thousand miles, or years, of that spot (85).

"The Happy Hedonist" is about a former English schoolmaster who has been lured by the writings of Robert Louis Stevenson to the Pacific in search of paradise. A manic-depressive who flees from one failed Eden to another, he is "forever hopeful despite all disillusionment" (123). The tone throughout is one of amused affection for this unnamed seeker of happiness in out-of-the-way places. Hall's amusement is based on more than an appreciation of the keen wit of this island-hopping malcontent, just as his fondness has a broader foundation than a mere regard for the intelligence, learning, and command of language displayed in the "hedonist's" letters to a friend which are the basis for Hall's sketch. Here is a man who embodies one set of Hall's values—a yearning for a peaceful realm remote from tumultuous industrial centers. But he conspicuously lacks those qualities that had saved Hall from some of his own more madcap impulses—common sense, an ability to bend with circumstances, and a capacity for extracting enjoyment from the real world without relinquishing his vision of an ideal one. But despite the disapproval he nearly always expresses for monomaniacs, Hall finds this always disappointed but always hopeful wanderer's objectives so congenial that he comments: "I hope that he has not abandoned his quest" (125). That hope, however, has not prevented Hall from finding the perpetual dreamer's perpetual disillusionment intrinsically ridiculous or from marveling at one point that the man has fled from an island that Hall himself has found especially beautiful.

"Prairie Winter" expresses Hall's belief in the futility of trying to impose his own will on the creative process. It is one of his many short works which begin as nostalgic recreations of boyhood experiences and end on wistful notes. In this instance the recollection revolves about an itinerant stranger who lodges briefly in a room above the clothing store in "Prairie Hills" where Hall is a clerk. The wanderer attempts to foster the young man's fondness for poetry by introducing him to a wide variety of verse. One day, while the two are walking together, a line comes into Hall's head: "Like hissing foam the windy withered grasses crawl" (143). He promises the stranger that he will finish the poem. But after years of trying, he is compelled to acknowledge his failure. Hall's point is that inspiration cannot be turned on by a mere assertion of will. The wise man, he implies, accepts the limitations nature imposes upon his power whatever disappointment or even shame such acceptance will entail.

"Under the Arctic Circle" is one of the few tangible products of Hall's most spectacular failure to impose his will upon his creative processes—his trip to Iceland. It will be recalled that his avowed purpose for going there was to write a book that he was never able to produce. This sketch effectively states one of Hall's favorite themes, the despoilment of nature by industrial civilization. The setting is a stark arctic landscape. Just as Hall is beginning to feel in harmony with it, a car intrudes upon his reverie. His mood is smashed beyond restoration when the driver announces himself to be an American who is bringing hydroelectric power to what he regards as a dismal backwash.

The next four selections are entertaining but so slight that they need not be given much attention here. In the first of them, "Glamorous Places," Hall reiterates a point he has often made—that an artist makes actual places more glamorous and more "real." The specific works he cites are Conrad's *Lord Jim*, Cather's *My Antonia*, and Robert Louis Stevenson's "A Lodging for the

Night." The following story, "Leviticus Redivivus," is a clever tid-bit about how, on a remote atoll where the natives pride themselves on having memorized large portions of the Bible, Hall, in order to save face, recites "A Capital Ship for an Ocean Trip" and tells them it is the eleventh chapter of Leviticus in English. "Some Island Grandmothers," a pastiche of two sketches in the *Woman's Home Companion*, involves some elderly women he encountered on various isolated islands.[16] In "A Person from Porlock" he makes a witty but spirited plea for an author's right to privacy. He then con-fesses that once, while cycling through Kent, he almost imposed himself on Joseph Conrad but fortunately lost his nerve before ac-tually knocking on the door of the "greatest artist of our time."

While hardly a miracle of profundity, "Settling Down in Polynesia" provides an interesting glimpse of the personalities of Hall and Nordhoff. "C. B." (Nordhoff's first two initials) is, of course, the more practical of the pair. Fearing that if they continue their vagrant ways they will end up in a dreary pension in Paris or in an old men's home in the United States, he insists the time has come to acquire permanent homes. As they roam about the un-named island (obviously Tahiti) in search of domiciles, they en-counter an English planter who warns them against remaining in the South Seas, citing the emptiness of his own life as a cautionary example. Later, however, they meet another English resident who is delighted with the island. The man is an ardent student of the language and folkways of the natives, but even he concludes that life in the South Pacific is not for everybody. After some other in-cidents the sketch concludes with Hall and his friend still undecided about "settling down"—"Therefore, we wandered on, in the midst of a multitude of small, delightful adventures. By the way, we didn't much care whether we made it or not" (254). In actuality, Nordhoff had more than "made it" long before 1923, when these sentences first appeared in print. And by 1928, when *Mid-Pacific* was published, Hall himself, now a husband and father, had settled in the Arué district of Tahiti, which was to remain his home for the rest of his life. But the insouciant, almost flippant ending, characteristic of Hall's humorous writings during these years, is ap-propriate to the exuberant mood of the piece. Yet the light treat-ment cannot obscure the fact that in "Settling Down in Polynesia" Hall presents a theme he develops with more heft elsewhere—the notion that even the most idyllic surroundings cannot make happy a man who lacks the proper inner resources.

"Tahiti's Coconut-Radio Service" begins with some amusing

anecdotes about the speed with which news passes from person to
person in Tahiti and ends with a paean to the tranquility of life in
Polynesia.

The final selection, "Public Benches and Public Benching,"
however, denounces the frenetic mode of life in Hall's native land.
In fact, in this broadside attack on American dynamism Hall tilts
not only at his old ogre, Henry Ford, but at one of his own idols,
Thoreau. The framework for this assault is an anecdote-laced discussion of the dearth of public benches in cities throughout the
United States. For Hall this deficiency is symptomatic of the
Americans' distrust of contemplation and reverie. So pervasive is
this distrust that even as reflective a man as Thoreau was corrupted
by it. Thus Thoreau converted contemplation itself into a strenuous
activity. Hall asserts, though, that *Walden* owes its charm to
Thoreau's having been as "passively receptive to the quality of day
as Walden Pond itself" (293).

Hall in effect says: if American pressure to strive can coerce even
a nature-loving philosopher to make the simple act of looking at a
woodland scene an intellectual gymnastic feat, who can be sur-
prised that the same pressure has culminated in the rape of nature
by machine-loving entrepreneurs like Henry Ford? In this selection
Hall provides a poignant example of the kind of defilement of the
land Ford's values can result in. Once, he tells us, while sitting on a
bench in a niche between two giant buildings in an ugly, bustling
Midwestern city, he met an old man whose family had once farmed
there. The man said he had returned home to sell a plot of ground
his father had once intended using as a family burial place. He then
showed the property to Hall; it was hidden behind a huge sign
which read: "SEVEN THOUSAND MORE SINCE
YESTERDAY—FORD." The ground itself, Hall reports, "Looked
sour and oily, and was littered with old brickbats and scraps of
paper torn from billboards" (286).

The reader may recall that a similar sign had horrified Hall on a
visit to his hometown of Colfax just after World War I. Now, like a
rampant eczema, the work of Ford and his competitors was
blighting the face of America. And the American love of ceaseless
activity left the nation helpless to resist the damage being done. Ah,
but there was always Tahiti for Hall himself. And so the sketch and
Mid-Pacific itself conclude with Hall's returning to his tranquil
South Sea island where people are not afraid of being branded as indolent; where vistas are not defaced by billboards; and where the

air is not rank with carbon monoxide. But even there he finds ominous discords. As he wanders through Papeete in a "trancelike mood" while the natives are taking their siestas, he is disturbed by the watchful eyes of Chinese vendors. The reader is thus left assuming that if those street peddlers cannot close their eyes to the possibility of making a sou or two, surely the far-ranging eyes of Henry Ford will soon focus themselves on Tahiti.

CHAPTER 5

A Partnership Resumed

H ALL may never have abandoned his conviction that the essay is the finest of literary genres. But by the late 1920s he had learned that it and its kindred forms were not very lucrative. Although his stipend from Sedgwick and Smith and the publication of his articles in the *Atlantic* and elsewhere had sustained him for several years, they had not given him financial security. Neither had the issuance of *On the Stream of Travel* and *Mid-Pacific*. However much Hall despised those who lived primarily for money, he realized he himself could not live without it even in Tahiti. Consequently, the temptation to wed his fortunes to those of his erstwhile partner must have been irresistible when Nordhoff asked him to collaborate on a boys' book about the Lafayette Flying Corps. After all, *Faery Lands of the South Seas*, their one previous commercial venture together, had done well. What is more, Nordhoff's two solo efforts in the juvenile line, *The Pearl Lagoon* and *The Derelict*, had demonstrated that there was a substantial demand for such fare.

Hall's motives for reviving the partnership are self-evident. Nordhoff's may appear to be less so. But aside from a desire to help an old friend, he must have wished to avail himself of phases of Hall's war experiences, such as imprisonment in Germany, absent from his own. Then, too, he may have sensed that certain aspects of Hall's temperament and talents compensated for deficiencies in his own, and vice versa.

Whatever their motives, the two men labored for nine months on *Falcons of France*. At their daily work sessions they developed the plan of composition they were to follow throughout their long partnership. Instead of keeping their contributions distinct as they had done in *Faery Lands of the South Seas*, they now made every effort to blend their work. To that end, they mapped out the plot in advance, then divided up the material. Nordhoff wrote the opening chapters, as he was usually to do, partly because his penchant for fast pacing would get the book off to an appropriately brisk start but also because, in this specific case, *Falcons of France* was a sequel to his own *The Pearl Lagoon*. Thus Nordhoff provides the first view of the hero, Charles Selden, as well as Selden's young friend, Gordon Forbes. Thereupon, in chapters four through eight Hall takes the men into action. The next chapter is Nordhoff's, the next three Hall's; four more by Nordhoff prepare for the three by Hall dealing with Selden's captivity and escape; then Nordhoff ties it all up in the final chapter.[1]

Yet such a résumé gives an erroneous impression. The two writers were in constant consultation with each other, one frequently amending the other's efforts. Moreover, they would often encroach on one another's territory since Nordhoff's specialties, not surprisingly, were description and exposition. To be sure, there were in this, their first collaborative attempt at fiction, some rough transitions, but these were smoothed over by judicious cutting on the part of their editor at Atlantic-Little, Brown, Edward Weeks. For better or worse, in sickness and in health, the two had become, at least in print, one.

I   A War Novel

Submitting *Falcons of France,* a book written for juveniles, to careful scrutiny may seem like making a probing analysis of a Nancy Drew mystery. Yet we cannot be too perfunctory with the fledgling effort at fiction of the soon-to-become-famous pair. There is no need, moreover, to patronize this rousing account of the Lafayette Flying Corps because it could be read with pleasure or profit by anyone, of any age, interested in its subject matter.

Essentially, *Falcons of France* is a *Bildungsroman* which carries Charles Selden from his father's ranch in California to the Lafayette Flying Corps and thence to a series of aerial combats which culminate with his becoming a German prisoner of war. Then, after a danger-strewn escape to Switzerland, he learns that the armistice has been signed and returns to Paris. There he and his friend Gordon Forbes decide to head for the South Seas. In a sense, therefore, Selden starts off as Nordhoff (the California background) and ends as Hall (the prisoner-of-war experience) with numerous adventures in between of the sort which befell both men during the war.

The attitude toward warfare throughout the work is no less ambivalent than it had been in Hall's own earlier war books,

Kitchener's Mob and *High Adventure*. On the one hand the conflict, or at least the aerial phase of it, is a great adventure for Selden
and never ceases to be so even after the brutalities of battle have
dimmed some of the glamour of combat. A large part of that
glamour derives from Selden's sheer joy in soaring through space.
But combat, too, produces its exaltation. Once, when Selden sees a
German Fokker with machine guns ablaze, he becomes positively
ecstatic. As the book progresses, however, there are frequent
references to the savagery of war scattered throughout portions
written by both Hall and Nordhoff. Selden becomes most acutely
aware of the butchery being endured by the infantry when his plane
crashes near the trenches. The fact that this episode, which closely
parallels one in Hall's *High Adventure*, appears in one of
Nordhoff's chapters is evidence of how fully the two authors
were able to integrate their efforts as well as of how much in accord
they were in their attitudes toward the war.

Another matter on which Hall and Nordhoff seem to have agreed
is martial fanaticism. Both consistently depict members of the
Lafayette Flying Corps as courageous (as indeed they were!), and
both exhibit respect for honest patriotism. But both also reveal a
distaste for combatants on either side who allow their zeal to make
them needlessly cruel or unchivalrous toward the enemy. In fact,
Falcons of France is admirably lacking in jingoism. When Selden is
shot down, his captors treat him humanely, as they treated Hall,
who wrote this section of the book. Nordhoff, for his part, exhibits a
distaste for the zealousness of a super ace named Tommy Slater.
This small, frail, normally gentle boy, who becomes a veritable
homicidal maniac whenever he gets behind the controls of his pursuit plane, appears in chapters by Hall as well as by Nordhoff. It is
in Nordhoff's, however, that he is developed most fully and in
which the young fire-eater's callousness emerges most forcefully. It
is also in one of Nordhoff's sections that Selden's friend Forbes
makes the observation after Slater's death that their young comrade
proved that people can combine good and bad qualities. This
remark is no doubt less than Socratic in profundity but is well above
the philosophical level generally encountered in such fiction. It is
also a remark with which Hall certainly agreed, whether or not
Nordhoff wrote it without consulting him. After all, Hall's own
sympathetic yet critical depictions of Crichton and the "Happy
Hedonist" in *Mid-Pacific* suggest comparably ambivalent feelings

toward compulsive men with mitigating decent impulses.

Both authors also exhibit throughout *Falcons of France* an antipathy toward pedantic or arbitrary authorities. The officers of the Lafayette Flying Corps are all splendid fellows who wink at minor infractions. The men themselves are, to put it mildly, selective in obeying orders, but good old Lieutenant de Gazic usually contrives to keep them out of trouble. As for Selden's German captors, they win their prisoner's approval when they prove to be not at all "Prussian" but, in the main, amiable sorts who will bend a regulation when necessary.

The final chapter suggests a possible difference between the two men which was to become more significant in their next book, *Mutiny on the Bounty.* Hall was no more enamored of insignia-wearing, office-holding bullies than Nordhoff was. In his own works, however, he usually avoids the type. The few such creatures who do appear, whether they are treated comically like the swaggering former captain in *Mid-Pacific* or seriously like the high priest of Koro in *The Far Lands*, are likely to be confounded either by their own mistakes or by the workings of fate. Nordhoff was more partial to the sock on the jaw or the grand, unequivocal gesture of defiance. Thus, when in Nordhoff's concluding chapter the heroic chauffeur, Flingot, while celebrating the end of the war is menaced by a spoilsport policeman, the chauffeur contemptuously thumbs his nose and drives off.

But, although such an ending would have been uncharacteristic, Hall probably could have written it. No episode in *Falcons of France*, in fact, seems indelibly marked with the authorship of either Nordhoff or Hall. One reason why they could merge their efforts so successfully is that they were drawing upon a fund of recollections in which they had much in common. Then, too, Charles Selden is so representative of all adventure-seeking enlistees that the two veterans of the Lafayette Flying Corps could readily identify with him. The loose organization of the plot, moreover, allowed each sufficient latitude to inject his own memories about the corps into the book without tearing apart its structure. Finally, they were able to achieve stylistic homogeneity because neither had an idiosyncratic style. Although Hall would sometimes shift into a Conradian lushness when a lyrical mood seized him, he usually wrote clear, straightforward, functional prose. So did Nordhoff. The two men, therefore, demonstrated in *Falcons of*

France that, at least as long as they were willing to keep their main character simple and their plot line flexible, they could merge their identities on paper.

II   *Two Solo Flights*

Nordhoff and Hall were soon to produce their most successful collaborative effort, *Mutiny on the Bounty*. But in 1930, the year after the appearance of *Falcons of France*, two books by Hall alone were published, *Mother Goose Land* and *Flying With Chaucer*. As its title indicates, the first of these was written for small children. Whimsical and fantastic, it offers at its best a Lewis Carroll-like topsy-turvy inventiveness. At one point, for instance, some characters take off their roller skates when they reach a downgrade because what is up for them is down for an earthling like the young hero, Roger Avery, who has been transported to the land of nursery rhymes by the cow that jumped over the moon. Elsewhere, when Roger suggests to three men who cannot keep up their stockings that they try braces, they reply scornfully that the rhyme to which they owe their existence will not permit them to. Throughout his stay, in fact, Roger keeps encountering arbitrary and absurd rules. At the same time, everyone he meets is either pleasant or harmlessly ridiculous. And so, when he is taken back to earth, he is sorry to be home until the cow tells him he can return whenever he wishes.

It would be going too far to regard *Mother Goose Land* as Polynesia and Earth as Colfax, Iowa (or vice versa?). But Hall is obviously playing here, in symbols a child can respond to, with themes that pervade his autobiographical writings. In *Mother Goose Land*, too, there is an exile who returns home and, even though he finds the experience disappointing, return he must in body as in thought. But he learns he need not remain at home or anywhere else because he can always travel vicariously through literature. As for rules and authorities, they may often be silly, but in most cases the best course is merely to laugh at them.

Much of the foregoing summary would apply to *Flying With Chaucer*, an account of Hall's imprisonment in Landshut, Bavaria, and of his "escape" to Switzerland. In a sense, therefore, the work is a companion piece to his final chapters in *Falcons of France*. But, whereas he treats Selden's imprisonment and escape in a heroic mode, Hall depicts his own comically. Were it not for its later pages, this book could aptly be entitled *Stone Walls Do Not a*

Prison Make because the main theme of the opening portion is that literature can liberate an imaginative mind even when the body is confined. In Hall's case such a liberation occurred when, as camp librarian, he appropriated a volume of *The Canterbury Tales* and soon discovered that he had found "a sovereign remedy for prison-camp *ennui*."[2] The account of his imprisonment thereafter is part literary essay and part reminiscence.

The second portion of the book deals with his flight to Switzerland and subsequent return to France. Unlike Charles Selden, Hall did not need an elaborate escape plan. He merely walked out the front gate, thanks to his benefactor, the Inspector, who decided to let the men go after the armistice even though regulations required that they be released or exchanged through official channels. Hall and his comrades thereupon journeyed by train in their allied uniforms to Lake Constance, where they traveled by boat to Romanshorn in Switzerland. Ironically, there they were promptly arrested by Swiss authorities. Soon released, they had a sumptuous dinner at the Hotel Bellevue, but the meal was marred by an atmosphere of international hatred. Back in France Hall joined a wild victory celebration made still wilder by generous libations of "demon alcohol." In narrating the incident, Hall pauses to take a swipe at Prohibition: "What a delightful demon he can be when treated as he would like to be treated: not as a bosom friend, but only as an occasional companion" (46). Hall then took a farewell solo flight across the Western Front, reliving in his imagination his war experiences.

The book concludes with Hall in Papeete contemplating his battered copy of Chaucer and observing that he had carried it over the battlefields of France and had read it by candlelight under the Arctic Circle as well as in "shadows of coconut palms . . . on lonely islands of the South Seas" (55). Once again, therefore, we find Hall juggling past and present, reality and imagination. And even in this work, where we would least expect to find it, Iowa intrudes and with it thoughts of home and family. At one point Hall writes: "Let me tell you, then, that I have a sense of family that none of the Halls up to my time, seem to have had, or the Youngs, my mother's people. Like many of the families of Middle-Western America who, toward the fifties of the last century peopled the prairies of the Mississippi Valley, we know almost nothing of our actual antecedents beyond our grandparents, and little enough concerning them" (19). How strange it is that this sense of family—yes, and of the land of his own family—should have burned so persistently in this self-exiled man! But for Hall reality was wherever his attention happened to be at the moment. And, thus, since his thoughts turned so often to Iowa, he was never really away from home for long.

CHAPTER 6

The Bounty *Trilogy*

T HE *Bounty* trilogy may owe its existence to Hall's retrospective cast of mind. After having rejected Nordhoff's
suggestion that they write another boys' book, Hall began looking
for a new subject. Suddenly, in a small volume he had purchased in
Paris during the war, he found it. When Nordhoff read Sir John
Barrow's account of the *Bounty* mutiny published in 1831, he too
became enthusiastic over the fictional possibilities of the famous insurrection. And it is no wonder that he did. The account of the ill-
fated voyage to get breadfruit plants for the West Indies was, as he
said to Hall, a "natural" for a historical novel—especially one
written by these two men, containing as the story did all the
elements with which they were most comfortable: A South Sea setting, a clash between freedom and authority, an interplay between
primitive and civilized peoples, and a multiplicity of exciting incidents. But, always less sanguine than his partner, Nordhoff soon
persuaded himself that the kind of book they envisioned "must
have been written long since." [1]

Ever the optimist, Hall was not to be daunted so readily. Off
went a letter of enquiry to the Bishop Museum in Honolulu. And
back came the encouraging news that the subject was all but untouched. The only published version, aside from Barrow's factual
one and accounts by seamen involved at least tangentially in the
mutiny or its complicated aftermath, was *Aleck, the Last of Mutineers, or, The History of Pitcairn Island*, an anonymous work for
children published in 1845 and "made up of a compilation culled
from other books, of the facts then known about the *Bounty*
mutiny." [2]

As the two men progressed further into the project, Ellery
Sedgwick, editor of the *Atlantic*, once more became their benefactor. Through Sedgwick's offices, they acquired the services of a
retired British naval officer, Captain Truefell, who sent to Tahiti

65

from London detailed descriptions of the *Bounty*. They also received from London copies of Admiralty records concerning the voyage, the mutiny, and the court-martial proceedings against the mutineers.

And so, there in the South Seas, surrounded by a vast store of old records, the team set to work. One of their earliest and most important decisions was not to relate the entire story in a single book. Their first volume would deal with the mutiny. Then, if that work succeeded, they would write a pair of sequels—one about Captain Bligh's open-boat voyage in the *Bounty*'s launch, and the other about the fate of Fletcher Christian, the leader of the mutiny, and the men who went with him to Pitcairn Island.

Once having acquired their source material and having limited their subject, they proceeded to write *Mutiny on the Bounty* in much the same manner in which they had produced *Falcons of France*. After contriving their plot and selecting their characters, they divided up segments of the tale between them, constantly consulting each other and frequently amending one another's work as they progressed. According to Edward Weeks, their editor, the entire opening portion up to the mutiny was to be written by Nordhoff. Hall would then take up the story at that point and would also be responsible for "the mutineers' return to Tahiti and the succession when they began to quarrel among themselves under Christian's leadership; he would describe the arrival of the *Pandora*, the ship which was sent from London to capture the mutineers; he would tell of its shipwreck and the eventual court-martial of the survivors, and the execution and the ending."[3]

The manuscript in the Grinnell College Library indicates that they more or less adhered to this plan. The chapter before the outbreak of the mutiny, however, was written on the same typewriter as the sections which Weeks attributes to Hall. Hence, it too is probably Hall's work. But perhaps we should not make too much of the importance of the division. As Weeks has observed, once the actual writing had begun, "these boundaries tended to disappear."[4] In fact, they disappeared so much that Ellery Sedgwick, who knew both men intimately, confessed that, although he possessed a copy which identified the chapters of each author, he was "powerless to distinguish between their contributions."[5] We must give *some* attention, nevertheless, when analyzing the novel, to who wrote what, while never forgetting that *Mutiny on the Bounty* was, in the truest sense, a collaborative achievement.

I *The Trilogy Launched*

It is unlikely that many people who have read it would deny that *Mutiny on the Bounty* is one of the best books of its kind ever written. But what kind of book is it? Cultivated readers would probably characterize it as melodrama. And in numerous respects they would be correct. Nordhoff and Hall's novel shares with the Western, the crime thriller, and the soap opera such features as a stark contrast between good and evil, sudden reversals, a portentous tone, and a dire sequence of events moving logically toward disaster only to swerve at the very end toward a happy resolution. Some of these features it also shares with Goethe's *Faust*, Dostoevski's novels, *Wuthering Heights*, and even *War and Peace*. It would be absurd, of course, to equate *Mutiny on the Bounty* with *Faust* or *War and Peace*. But a careful reading of Nordhoff and Hall's book reveals that a finely wrought popular work with melodramatic elements can have its subtleties, complexities, and can even produce something akin to catharsis.

Especially admirable is the use to which Nordhoff and Hall put their extensive research. For the purposes of plot or even of characterization they need not have looked beyond Sir John Barrow's marvelous book. In slightly more than three hundred pages, Barrow covered not merely the major events surrounding the *Bounty*'s voyage, the mutiny, the court-martial, and the Pitcairn Island story, but he also presented his facts with a justice to all, particularly admirable in view of his position as Secretary of the British Admiralty. Of course he condemned the mutiny. But, while citing Bligh's undeniable merits, he made no attempt to palliate his less attractive qualities—his nasty temper, his abusive tongue, and his vindictiveness. Barrow was equally severe in his judgment of Captain Edwards, the commander of the *Pandora*, the ship which took back to England the mutineers and their innocent companions who had remained behind in Tahiti after Christian had set sail in search of a more remote hiding place. Barrow even provided Nordhoff and Hall with their narrator, because he gave an extended and sympathetic account of Peter Heywood, the midshipman who served as a model for Roger Byam.

But what Barrow alone could not have given them was that feeling for specifics which permeates *Mutiny on the Bounty*—specifics about how the *Bounty* looked, about its layout, what the men ate, drank, and wore; specifics about English ports, prisons, and laws.

Such accuracy of detail often imparts a sense of reality to incidents which, however historical, sometimes border on the incredible. Yet much of the effectiveness of the book is due to the selectivity with which Nordhoff and Hall employed those details. There are no lengthy descriptions and no digressions crammed with data. Specifics are injected sparingly—frequently enough to heighten verisimilitude but never intrusively enough to impede the narrative flow.

Two examples of such restraint (both from one of Hall's chapters) must suffice. In one, Roger Byam is waiting on the deck of his prison ship to be transported to his court-martial aboard H.M.S. *Duke*: "Shortly before eight o'clock we saw a long boat, with a guard of marines in dress uniform, put off from the great ship's side and approach the *Hector*, and on the stroke of the hour a solitary gun was fired from the *Duke*. It was a signal for the court-martial. Our time had come."[6] Here, precise details such as the exact time and the firing of a solitary gun not merely enhance vividness but actually seem to move the story along. A few paragraphs later Hall writes: "During the first day's proceedings we were compelled to stand, but owing to the length of the trial, a bench was later provided for us" (286). This detail, offered almost as an aside, says more about the ordeal of the men than pages of exposition might have done, yet it is also a good realistic touch.

Nordhoff and Hall are similarly adroit in providing a historical context for the mutiny. The seizure of the *Bounty* occurred on April 27, 1789, less than seven years after the Battle of Yorktown had ended the American Revolutionary War and less than three months before, on July 14, the fall of the Bastille would precipitate a far bloodier upheaval in Europe. The authors, again trusting their superb story to do its work, do not burden their readers with allusions to events in France or distort history to underscore parallels between the overthrowing of Bligh and the toppling of the Bourbon monarchy. Yet linkages between the two assaults on established authority are made in the very first sentence when Roger Byam lauds his fellow Englishmen, the principal foes of Revolutionary France, for their dislike of change.

Another yoking of the French Revolution and the mutiny occurs a few pages later. Commenting on his boyhood yearning to go to the South Seas, Byam explains that early accounts of Polynesia "excited an interest almost inconceivable to-day." He then attributes the widespread interest in the Pacific to the popularity of

Rousseau's doctrine that man was happiest and most virtuous when free from the laws and institutions of civilization. Such ideas, Byam asserts, were shortly to have "lamentable and far-reaching results"—revolution (7).

Byam's opinions about such matters are of more than peripheral importance because he is not simply the narrator. In fact, it is around him that the plot pivots. Bligh vanishes in Chapter Nine to reappear only briefly in the epilogue. Christian makes his exit in Chapter Eleven, less than halfway to the end of this twenty-seven-chapter work, and is not seen again. Thereafter the focus of interest is on Byam's arrest, trial, and acquittal. Even the events leading up to the mutiny serve, in purely structural terms, as a preparation for Byam's decision not to support it despite his sympathy for Bligh's victims and his detestation of Bligh's harshness. *Mutiny on the Bounty* is thus the story of a young conservative who decides that, although all is not well with his world, order must be preserved. After being condemned to death by his superiors, he is pardoned at the last moment. He thereupon returns to the navy, serves with distinction, and finally becomes a captain.

The foregoing is essentially what happened to Byam's historical prototype, Peter Heywood. Now, of course, by choosing Heywood as the model for their protagonist, Nordhoff and Hall in a sense converted events which were tragic for most of the participants into a success story. Of the eight men who sailed off with Christian on the *Bounty*, only Alexander Smith survived the bloody events on Pitcairn Island. Of the sixteen who remained on Tahiti, two died there, four perished in the wreck of the *Pandora*, three were later hanged, and seven were either acquitted or pardoned. Of those who escaped the hangman's rope, Heywood alone went on to live a long and prosperous life. Morrison, the gunner's mate, lost his life in a naval engagement not long after being pardoned. The others—Muspratt, Norman, Colman, McIntosh, and Byrne—sank into obscurity.

Yet, although their decision to concentrate on Heywood was to opt for melodrama over tragedy, Nordhoff and Hall's approach to the story was probably the wisest they could have chosen given their talents, their experience, their method of composition, and their philosophies. Both authors, to begin with, were most comfortable with first-person narration, having used it extensively in the works they had produced individually as well as in *Falcons of France*. They had also demonstrated a partiality to the initiation-story pattern in which a young man from the provinces would come to maturity after a set of new and trying experiences. Heywood was, in many respects, a real-life, eighteenth-century counterpart of Charles Selden, the hero of Nordhoff and Hall's earlier book—a bright young man who enlisted in a military organization in search of adventure. He offered the further advantage of having been in a position to observe a wider range of events than any other man aboard the *Bounty*. He was also callow enough for both of the two highly individual mature writers to identify with him as they could never have done with more complex, more idiosyncratic figures like Bligh and Christian. Yet he was reflective and literate enough for Nordhoff and Hall to use him on occasion as a mouthpiece for some of their own ideas about authority, revolution, and the South Seas.

After stating in the opening chapters his Tory predilections as well as, somewhat incongruously, his fondness for books depicting the South Pacific as a new Eden, Byam becomes throughout the next seven chapters principally a set of eyes and ears. No sooner is he in uniform than he witnesses a sailor being flogged to death. Afterward, at dinner the high-ranking officers, while savoring their victuals, express approval of such severities, and none approves more heartily than Captain Bligh.

Thereafter, through the next six chapters, Bligh demonstrates that he is a man who practices his principles. The *Bounty*'s voyage becomes a nightmare of beatings, imprisonments in the hold, and assorted harangues and harassments relieved only by an idyllic interlude in Tahiti while the ship is being loaded with saplings of breadfruit trees. The common seamen are not the only victims of Bligh's brutalities. He orders a midshipman, Edward Young, whipped on the quarter-deck for having failed to apprehend a deserter; he imprisons the ship's carpenter in irons; he so antagonizes the ship's master, Fryer, that the latter refuses to dine with the captain. Finally, Bligh precipitates a mutiny by publicly accusing Christian, whom he himself had recently promoted to second in command, of having stolen coconuts from the captain's private store. What makes the charge particularly offensive is that Bligh himself has been filching from the ship's supplies of cheese. Christian, on the other hand, is Bligh's antithesis—brave, generous, amiable, popular with officers and men alike. And Byam has every reason, looking back on these events many years later, to take a jaundiced view of the man whose testimony almost got him hanged and who wrote a gratuitously cruel letter to Byam's mother.

Byam's narration in these chapters, in fact, makes the mutiny seem both inevitable and justified. His frequent tendency to refrain from commenting on events merely damns Bligh all the more because the reported incidents, which invariably put the captain in the worst possible light, are thus presented with a semblance of objectivity. When Byam does have a good word to say for his commander, the compliment promptly turns into denigration: "Had his character in other respects been equal to his courage, his energy, and his understanding Bligh would to-day have a niche in history among the greatest seamen of England" (87 - 88). The statement is feeble praise indeed in view of what Byam has already revealed about the character of the captain. Even occasional comments about generally deplorable conditions throughout the British navy do not mitigate the case against Bligh. Their overall effect is to suggest that if all those veteran seamen, having endured floggings and bad food on other ships, hate Bligh so intensely then he must be dreadful. And Byam from time to time strengthens that effect with a verbal nudge, such as entitling Chapter Four "Tyranny" or informing us that the flogging of Midshipman Young is "almost without precedent in the Service" (61).

But, although the first eight chapters lucidly and briskly prepare for the uprising, they do little to foreshadow Byam's instant and unequivocal refusal to support the mutineers led by his good friend Christian. At least Peter Heywood, according to Barrow's account of the court-martial, was confused during the turmoil on deck. Heywood, moreover, chose to remain on board rather than to join Bligh in the launch as the "lesser of two evils."[7] But Byam, Heywood's fictional counterpart, not only unhesitatingly resolves to resist but plans to recapture the ship and is finally prevented from accompanying Bligh by sheer bad luck.

This dearth of foreshadowing, however, is not a blunder on the part of Nordhoff and Hall. On the contrary, it is the master stroke of the novel. The remainder of the book becomes, in effect, a vindication of Byam's seemingly perverse decision. No sooner are the mutineers in control of the *Bounty* than they begin quarreling among themselves. And, even though Christian is a natural leader, he is no longer a legitimate one; consequently, his authority shows signs of eroding from the start, thus portending the anarchy that will destroy all but one of the men who go with him to Pitcairn Island. Conversely, the legitimate commander, Bligh, transformed into a superb leader by dire circumstances, safely conducts his launch across the Pacific in one of the greatest feats in maritime history. So remarkable is his achievement that Byam, under the threat of death because of Bligh's accusations against him, concedes that Bligh alone could have performed such a deed. As for Byam's faith in British justice, it is ultimately vindicated when the innocent men are either acquitted or, like himself and Morrison, pardoned as Heywood was.

Just as events from Chapter Nine to the end of the book justify Byam's decision, the portrait of him in those pages explains it. In fact, long before the epilogue, his refusal to support the mutineers has come to seem in retrospect as inevitable as the first eight chapters had made the mutiny appear. As the novel progresses, it becomes increasingly clear that Byam could not have supported any massive assault on authority and order because he is what today might be called a "square." He has the square virtues of a sense of duty, devotion to work, and loyalty to country, family, and friends (in just about that order). He also has the square vices of stolidness and primness. Byam, however, is a square who instinctively hates bullies and who sympathizes with their victims. He is, in addition, one who sometimes seems to yearn to become an eighteenth-century prototype of the South Sea beachcomber.

Because Byam is most dominant in Hall's chapters, it is tempting to regard him as Hall's persona. But the temptation should be resisted. To be sure, Byam's antipathy toward change, his retrospective cast of mind, his attachment to his rural birthplace, and his optimism make his attitudes, although hardly his chilly personality, seem like Hall's. Furthermore, some of Byam's remarks about the South Seas duplicate ones Hall was to attribute to himself in *Under a Thatched Roof* in a record of a conversation with Nordhoff—remarks with which Nordhoff took issue. In essence Hall there defended South Sea lotus-eating, rambling, and reverie. Nordhoff denounced all three and praised a more active kind of life. At the same time his tone was pessimistic and even cynical, whereas Hall's was sanguine.

Thus Byam sounds very much like Hall when he says: "Worry over the future is without doubt the white man's greatest strength and greatest weakness in his quest of happiness—the only conceivable object in life" (182). He sounds even more so when he decides to adopt, at least during his sojourn in Tahiti, the "tropical philosophy" which he defines as putting the "past and future out of mind" (189). The problem is that even though such statements are nearer to Hall's views than to Nordhoff's, they appear in Nordhoff's chapters. Conversely, it is in one of Hall's sections that Byam, while imprisoned on the *Pandora,* strikes the bullying Lieutenant Parkin—his one piece of forthright action of the sort Nordhoff so admired.

What these facts prove, of course, is not that either author badgered the other into writing passages that went against his grain, but that Byam's words and deeds were determined largely by his functions in a story line that the two writers had hammered out together. In order to participate in such a wide spectrum of incidents and be credible in his account of them, he has to be adventurous enough to set off for the South Seas but cautious enough and patriotic enough not to join the mutiny; educated enough to be writing the book and sufficiently well born to have friends powerful enough to obtain his pardon, but ignorant enough of the navy to be shocked by its code; fond enough of Polynesian life to get involved with it but not so fond that he would succumb to an urge to return to Tahiti after his pardon rather than reenlist in the navy—and so on. It is astounding that a character who is so obviously a device coheres at all, let alone emerges in this collaborative work with some kind of identity.

No less remarkable is it that Nordhoff and Hall were able to achieve a stylistic homogeneity while avoiding a jarring sense of anachronism. Although no reader familiar with eighteenth-century literature is likely to be under the impression that he is reading an authentic manuscript of the period, neither is he apt to be painfully aware that he is *not* reading one. There is also none of that disconcerting clash between narrative prose and dialogue that often mars historical fiction, a fact all the more extraordinary when one recalls that statements made by characters in *Mutiny on the Bounty* were sometimes taken verbatim from contemporary records.

The question remains to be answered: what kind of work is *Mutiny on the Bounty?* Of its melodramatic elements we have already spoken. But melodrama is more a mode of development than a genre. "Historical novel" seems an apt designation. Yet, for all its historicity and verisimilitude, the book possesses a quality normally lacking in realistic fiction, historical or otherwise. Years ago in his doctoral dissertation the author of this study referred somewhat disdainfully to the novel as a fairy tale. Having reexamined it with more mature and less patronizing eyes, he is now convinced that the essentially childlike view of the *Bounty*'s tragic story is a major source of the work's strength. This is no *Terry and the Pirates*, though, conjuring up silly escapist fantasies. What the book does, rather, is to take some of the most elemental fears and wishes many and perhaps most of us bear from our childhood years and project them upon a vast historical canvas without doing radical violence to history itself. Thus *Mutiny on the Bounty* is a hybrid which fuses fact and myth, realism and fantasy.

On the fantasy level Bligh is every bullying authority figure who has ever terrified a child—the sarcastic teacher, the officious principal, and—yes—the wicked stepfather. Christian is the good-natured, reckless older brother or stronger friend who we keep hoping will thrash the bully. At the same time, we realize that the brother-friend will suffer retribution if he actually strikes the tyrant because behind this odious authority figure stands the awesome, omnipotent structure of all authority everywhere. Thus Byam—not so much Everyman as Everyboy—cannot admit to having wished this punishment to befall his friend or brother. Yet the fact remains that Byam has hated Bligh and has certainly not wished him well. Indeed, his entire account of Bligh is a portrait of a man who deserves a sock on the jaw or a kick on the shins. And so, when the revolt comes, Byam must be punished because his heart has been full of disrespect for an authority figure. But he must ultimately be rescued because he is innocent of any word or deed that could even remotely be construed as rebellious. He knows it; his friends know it; God knows it; and—what amounts to almost the same thing—Sir Joseph Banks, President of the Royal Society and instigator of the *Bounty*'s voyage, knows it even though he cannot until the very end come up with exonerating evidence. Banks, in fact, is one of those benign figures so common in fairy tales—wise and loving but oddly obtuse when it comes to the machinations of the wicked stepmother (or, in this instance, wicked stepfather). But, when a missing midshipman from the *Bounty* shows up to corroborate a vital point in Byam's testimony, Banks secures a pardon for the innocent hero.

Now there is some historical basis for much of this. Peter Heywood was convicted and then pardoned. Heywood's reprieve, however, came much earlier in his progression toward the gallows. Then, too, his principal benefactor was not the great Sir Joseph but a more obscure man named Pasley. Furthermore, Heywood's case did not depend, as Byam's does, on incidents which could have been verified only by three missing persons, two of whom were dead. The court, having heard all the evidence including

Heywood's own lengthy and eloquent testimony, concluded that he was guilty in only the most technical sense, and, while deciding against him, recommended mercy.

Byam, however, is both more guilty than Heywood and more innocent—more involved, that is, through friendship and sympathy with the mutineers but less hesitant in his rejection of them when the mutiny transpires. He is also punished more terribly, coming closer to being hanged, than Heywood ever came. What is more, Byam, like Bligh but unlike Heywood, is a protégé of Banks, the prime mover of the voyage; consequently, Byam stands closer to the center of the story than Heywood stood.

What these shifts in emphasis accomplish is to make the mutiny and its aftermath the story of Byam's fears, sympathies, antipathies, sufferings, and final vindication. And, because he has some of that blankness which characterizes mythic heroes, he often functions less as a mask for Nordhoff and Hall than as a stand-in for readers youthful enough in spirit to identify with him. *Mutiny on the Bounty* thus provides such readers with the thrill of vicariously smashing all authority; then it first punishes and finally exculpates them for that thrill.

The view toward rebellion which pervades the book, therefore, is a conservative one. The novel suggests, in effect, that even though a tyrannical individual may deserve to be removed from power, a precipitous and illegal assault on constituted authority will cause more suffering than do the abuses which the assault was meant to eliminate. Certainly the mere facts of the *Bounty*'s voyage support such a view as, perhaps, do the facts about the French and Russian Revolutions. Hall's distaste for sudden changes of any kind has been demonstrated frequently throughout this study; so has his disapproval of single-minded, demonic-willed men. Thus no one should doubt that Byam speaks for Hall when, denouncing Christian for having instigated the mutiny, he says: "Men of such passionate nature, when goaded by injustice into action, lose all sense of anything save their own misery. They neither know nor care, until it is too late, what ruin they make of the lives of others" (141 - 42).

A final observation needs to be made about *Mutiny on the Bounty*. It would be unjust to Nordhoff and Hall to leave someone who has not read the book with the impression that they cheapen the terrible events surrounding the *Bounty*'s voyage by having their hero at the end sail off into the sunrise ready to fight for king and country, his heart athrob with forgiveness. In the epilogue, Byam

returns many years later to Tahiti. En route, while in Australia, he
briefly encounters Bligh who, as governor of New South Wales, has
become the central figure of another uprising. Byam discovers that
the old man, as irascible and overbearing as ever, has learned
nothing from his experiences. Moreover, Byam's return to Tahiti is
a melancholy experience. The place soon becomes for him a
"graveyard of memories." Worse, it has become a literal graveyard
where, because of pestilence, four-fifths of the population has perished in the valley in which he and Tehani had their idyll twenty
years earlier. To be sure, life goes on. Although Tehani is dead,
Byam's daughter by her survives, as does a granddaughter. But, as
he leaves the island, he reflects: "suddenly the place was full of
ghosts—shadows of men alive and dead—my own among them"
(379).

The book thus concludes on an appropriately disquieting note.
The incidents depicted in *Mutiny on the Bounty* have not suggested
that all is right with the world but that rebellions make bad conditions worse and that, in a free society like England's, justice will
prevail although perhaps only after long and painful delays. The
epilogue, moreover, indicates that Byam finally learns that,
however things turn out, the essential sadness of life remains: youth
perishes, lovely primitive cultures vanish or become tainted,
delights of the past slip away—hardly childish lessons.

II   *The Wake of the* Bounty

The reception of *Mutiny on the Bounty* must have surpassed
Hall's most sanguine expectations. It became a best-seller, a Book-
of-the-Month Club selection, the recipient of adulatory reviews,
and the source of a popular movie. The last point is not without
irony because Hall had written contemptuously of motion-picture
theaters and their patrons in *Mid-Pacific*. The irony was compounded when several other Nordhoff and Hall novels (*The
Hurricane*, *No More Gas*, *Men Without Country*, and *The High
Barbaree*) became celluloid epics and when *Mutiny on the Bounty*
became the source for a second, far more costly film production in
the early 1960s.

No one should assume, however, that between the completion of
Falcons of France in 1929 and the publication of *Mutiny on the
Bounty* in 1932 nothing of consequence happened to Hall. In addi-
tion to the two books discussed in Chapter Eight, both published in

1930, Hall wrote essays, sketches, and verse for periodicals, principally for the *Atlantic*. One of these, "At Forty-Five," is especially interesting. In it Hall confesses that in recent years he has lost his "social-and-political-mindedness" but contends that certain people such as himself function best within the confines of a narrow range of interest.[8] Although the essay is one of Hall's better efforts, he did not include it in his next collection of such works, *Under a Thatched Roof* (1942). Perhaps by the end of the decade, during which a depression had been succeeded by a world war, an apparent disdain for "social-and-political-mindedness" seemed misguided. But the work is by no means an expression of callous indifference to what was transpiring outside Tahiti. Its concluding sentences make it clear that just as Thoreau regarded Concord as a microcosm, Hall perceived Tahiti as a miniature version of the larger world. The other essays in the volume, moreover, deal with such a wide variety of subjects that no reader could assume that their author had been devoting most of his time to gaping vacant-mindedly at land crabs scuttling across tropical beaches.

As a matter of fact Hall was very active indeed throughout the 1930s producing during the decade five books with Nordhoff and four without him. And perhaps at no other time was he as busy as in the years immediately following the completion of *Falcons of France*. In addition to *Mutiny on the Bounty* and its two sequels, Hall and his partner wrote a play about the war, *The Empty Chair*, which Hall took to New York in search of a producer. He was, however, unable to find one other than a close friend whose money Hall refused to risk.

Despite this setback and the illness of his son, Conrad, which necessitated a trip to the Mayo Clinic, these were good years for Hall. Hard work was at last bringing him recognition. His monetary problems were to abate with the publication of the *Bounty* trilogy. In 1930 his daughter, Nancy, was born. But for Hall's partner the early 1930s were to mark the onset of a long decline.[9] The death of his son, Charles, followed by an ever-widening rift between his wife and himself no doubt contributed to his increasingly heavy drinking. Perhaps, too, because of his deeply ingrained pessimism, he was less able to savor success than Hall was.

Whatever the reasons, in these years the two men began to reverse their former roles. Nordhoff, who in the 1920s had seemed the more purposeful and disciplined, began to flounder. Hall, on the other hand, who had often been incapable of sustained effort, was to become increasingly the dominant partner after the publication of *The Hurricane* in 1936. But we shall discuss these matters in their proper place. Meanwhile we must examine the two sequels to *Mutiny on the Bounty*.

Although Nordhoff and Hall had done most of their work on *Pitcairn's Island* before starting *Men Against the Sea*, the latter book was published earlier because extensive revising delayed the appearance of *Pitcairn's Island*. This reversal in the originally planned sequence was fortunate. The events in *Men Against the Sea* are more integrally related to those in the first volume of the trilogy, *Mutiny on the Bounty*, than the incidents in *Pitcairn's Island* are. Nordhoff and Hall had recounted the main details of the story of Bligh's 3,618 mile open-boat voyage across the Pacific in *Mutiny on the Bounty* probably because its outcome had had such an impact on the fate of its protagonist, Roger Byam. On the other hand, they said nothing in the earlier book about the occurrences on Pitcairn Island because those events had no effect on Byam. [10] The proper place of *Men Against the Sea*, therefore, is between its two companion works.

In *Men Against the Sea* Bligh, the harsh master of the *Bounty*, becomes a heroic figure when confronted with responsibility for the lives of the nineteen men crammed into the small ill-supplied launch. Thus, whatever he might have done before or whatever he was to do later, he vindicates in this book the favorable opinion held of his abilities by Sir Joseph Banks, Captain Cook, and the British Naval High Command. A simple sense of justice may have prompted the authors to create such a laudatory portrait. Except for a few sentences of praise, Nordhoff and Hall had presented a relentlessly unfavorable picture of him in *Mutiny on the Bounty*. Yet Bligh's record was mixed. If his irascibility provoked mutiny, his courage, self-discipline, and indomitable will made him as effective a commander in combat during the Napoleonic wars as they made him during the voyage of the crowded launch across thousands of miles of treacherous water strewn with islands inhabited by fierce cannibals.

In rectifying their harsh picture of Bligh in *Mutiny on the Bounty*, Nordhoff and Hall went even further in praising him in *Men Against the Sea* than they had gone in vilifying him in the earlier novel. In fact, in *Men Against the Sea* the erstwhile quarter-deck tyrant is so wise and humane that the mutiny seems in retrospect incomprehensible. No crew would ever have risen up against such a benevolent commander—and no crew would have dared depose such a firm and resourceful one. Now, of course, the facts themselves suggest that the Bligh who provoked the mutiny was not altogether the same man as the one who took the launch and its starving crew safely to the Dutch East Indies. But altered circumstances could not have transformed him beyond recognition. Yet, whereas nothing in the earlier book had implied that Bligh lacked courage, determination, and competence, everything in *Men Against the Sea* makes it inconceivable that he could ever have resorted to the petty thievery or the gratuitous harassment of officers Nordhoff and Hall attribute to him in *Mutiny on the Bounty*.

These discrepancies, however, may have been less a result of the authors' desire to be fair to Bligh than of a reluctance to stray from contemporary accounts of the launch's voyage. In writing about the mutiny, they could choose between divergent versions—Bligh's on the one hand and on the other Morrison's journal, Heywood's letters, and records of the testimony of some of the mutineers. Of the incidents in the *Bounty's* launch, their only detailed sources were Bligh's published volume about the mutiny and his private journal. Both, needless to say, presented the commander of the *Bounty* in a favorable light. Evidently Nordhoff and Hall were unwilling to fabricate details that went counter to Bligh's account. Moreover, the collaborative nature of their project as well as the dictates of popular adventure fiction precluded a sustained and subtle internal portrait of the captain.

Having decided once more to write a first-person narrative, they chose the point of view of Thomas Ledward, the acting surgeon, who becomes in effect a ventriloquist's dummy for Bligh's self-serving version of the voyage. But, whereas Bligh's own book recounts the story with at least a pretense of modesty and objectivity, Nordhoff and Hall's Ledward is so adulatory that he often sounds downright sycophantic. His bias is clear at the outset when he says: "Knowing the necessity for strict discipline at sea, and the unruly nature of seamen as a class, I by no means considered that Captain Bligh's punishments exceeded in severity what the rules and necessities of the services demanded; nor had I believed the men themselves thought so."[11]

As the voyage proceeds, Ledward proffers a veritable litany of the captain's merits. Bravery and self-assurance we had been prepared to accept. His unwillingness to resort to guile to pacify a native chief comes as no great surprise. But, when we find him described as "cheerful, kindly, and considerate," we remain astonished even when Ledward assures that he would not have forseen the emergence of these traits to such a degree before the mutiny (94). On and on come revelations about Bligh's virtues. He is compassionate. He is even gentle. And when Purcell, one of the few men in the launch who evince hostility toward Bligh, assails the captain's character, Fryer, who aboard the *Bounty* had been so incensed at Bligh that he refused to dine with him, says: "But where would we be without him now? Tell me that. Whom would you wish in his place in the launch?" (162). Not content with attributing merely human virtues to Bligh, Ledward describes him in language appropriate to some half-divine epic hero, as in the following passage: "There was a blinding glare of lightning, followed by a peal of thunder that seemed to shake the very bed of the deep. At that moment a great sea flung the launch into an all but vertical position. And there sat Bligh as on a throne, exalted in more than a physical sense" (82).

Nordhoff and Hall, of course, could have reconciled their accounts of Bligh's tyranny aboard the *Bounty* with their portrait of his benignity in the launch by giving *Men Against the Sea* a narrator who is initially hostile to the captain but who gradually recognizes Bligh's merits. But this sort of slowly evolving change of perspective would probably have been unattainable by a team of writers working away at separate portions of the tale, regardless of how often they conferred with each other. And, had they used an omniscient narrator, they undoubtedly would have exposed the book to the disjointing shifts of tone that almost confounded their attempt to write *Pitcairn's Island*, where initially they did employ such a point of view. In subordinating their individual perceptions of Bligh to Ledward's unvarying idealization of him, Nordhoff and Hall were able to unify their efforts. They achieved this unity, however, at the expense of subtlety and sometimes, at least for the reader familiar with *Mutiny on the Bounty*, at the expense of credibility.

Yet, if read without reference to its predecessor, *Men Against the Sea* is a thoroughly satisfying adventure story. It moves along briskly. It depicts actions, people, and places vividly and economically. Since the only sustained conflict is the one indicated in the title—the clash between nature and the men in the launch—the book is inevitably more episodic than *Mutiny on the Bounty*, but the fact in no way abates the forward thrust of the work. The individual episodes are engrossing enough to pull the reader along In them Bligh and his subordinates are menaced by storms and doldrums, hostile savages, and the selfishness of some of the men in the boat. Yet always they survive, sometimes by apparent good luck, as when a tern alights on the bow to provide them with sorely needed sustenance. More often, however, Bligh is responsible for saving them. In every crisis he has the proper response: firmness when firmness is appropriate, gentleness when the men need to be comforted. Sometimes readers who pause to reflect may wish that Bligh would be human enough to make an error or two in judgment. Aboard the *Bounty* he was, at least in that regard, very human indeed.

Men Against the Sea gave its authors so little difficulty that they completed it in about two months. Writing *Pitcairn's Island*, however, proved such an ordeal that, after grinding out thirteen chapters, they sent off their abortive manuscript to Edward Weeks, who returned it with some advice that finally enabled them to finish the novel.

At first it appears surprising that *Pitcairn's Island* should have caused Nordhoff and Hall such acute birth pains. The actual Pitcairn story contained every element essential to either high tragedy or thrilling melodrama. It offered a gentleman officer who had become a renegade; a seized ship manned by cutthroat mutineers like Quintal, McCoy, and Williams; and a remote, deserted, all-but-unknown island where the fugitives sought refuge with their Polynesian wives. There they turned a paradise into a veritable hell. Men stole each other's wives and drank themselves into stupors; they killed themselves and murdered each other until only one mutineer remained alive. Finally, there was redemption: the sole surviving mutineer renounced drink, turned to the Bible, and taught the gospel to his own children and those of his dead companions. Here, in short, was a hero worthy of Conrad, an orgy of violence worthy of an Elizabethan dramatist, and a moral tale worthy of Tolstoy. Now, of course, Nordhoff and Hall would never have attempted to rival Conrad, Shakespeare, or Tolstoy. But this rich, varied, thrilling material contained elements perfectly suited to the interests of both of the partners. Surely even Nordhoff could not have wished for more action, villainy, or heroism. As for Hall, here he had an opportunity to exploit the themes most dear to him—solitude, Polynesian tranquility menaced by the white man's greed, and the ultimate goodness of mankind.

Perhaps their difficulty grew out of the fact that, while the Pitcairn material could readily be used to express the outlook of either Nordhoff or Hall, it could not be made to reflect the viewpoint of both men without distorting it considerably. One problem that plagued them was finding a narrative center. At first they attempted to relate the story from an omniscient point of view. But, as their book came to seem increasingly like a catalogue of horrors, they gave up and sent their fragmentary manuscript to Edward Weeks. Weeks proposed that they have Alexander Smith, the sole surviving mutineer on Pitcairn, tell parts of the story to the crew of the *Topaz*, the American ship which happened upon the island in 1808. Weeks suggested that Smith tell only of those events he observed before his wounding and argued that Smith's narration, having been softened "by time and loyalty" to his dead comrades, would not unduly stress the more sordid aspects of the story.[12] This advice helped Nordhoff and Hall to complete the novel, but it did not altogether resolve the problem of unifying the work. The shifts in point of view tended to fragment the book rather than to give it a Conradian complexity. A strong central character might have bound everything together the way Jim makes *Lord Jim* cohere. But Christian, who dominates the first part of *Pitcairn's Island*, dies halfway through the story. As for Smith, who narrates much of the concluding part, he tends to get lost among the horrendous incidents he relates.

Another problem, as Weeks's comments cited above indicate, was the plethora of violence. Weeks reports that Nordhoff, who disagreed with Hall about the matter, wanted to maximize the bloodshed and even went so far as to suggest in a letter that the st y "*should* be told . . . in a robust, bloody, and slightly pornographic Elizabethan fashion."[13]

The disagreement here between the partners represented, one suspects, more than a quibble over literary strategy. The sort of book Nordhoff envisioned might have been a better one. But Hall could not have contributed to it without having done considerable violence to many of his most firmly rooted convictions. The novel they actually wrote, therefore, may not be so much the result of a compromise with the tastes of female readers (as Nordhoff misogynistically implied) as of an imperfect compromise between the two authors—a compromise in which Hall got more than he gave but in which he did not get enough to make the work a completely satisfactory vehicle for his ideas.

Some of those ideas are difficult to reconcile with the events that actually transpired on Pitcairn. No talented writer determined to refute primitivism and to depict man as innately depraved would have had much trouble accommodating himself to those events. Hall, however, was anything but an antiprimitivist, and to the end of his life he insisted upon the essential goodness of man. Thus, whereas a Joseph Conrad or a William Golding might have emphasized the viciousness of all concerned, Polynesians as well as white men, Hall and his collaborator placed the onus on the English mutineers. This is not to say that the natives in *Pitcairn's Island* do not at times behave with savage ferocity. Such ferocity, however, is invariably provoked by the misdeeds of the white man. Gone, moreover, are many of the treacherous actions attributed to them by Captain F. W. Beechey, whose account of the events on Pitcairn Island is, as Harry L. Shapiro has observed, the most convincing of the many versions not merely because it is the most detailed but because it is the only one that incorporates passages from the now-lost diary of Edward Young.[14] In Beechey's version, in fact, nearly everyone on the island behaves abominably.[15] The whites are greedy, intolerant, and lustful. Those who are not brutal are cowardly, and some manage to be both. The Polynesians are little better. They are servile, furtive, and, at times, thoroughly barbaric.

Clearly much of this would never do for Hall and perhaps not even for Nordhoff. Does Beechey relate that the natives submitted to becoming slaves and resorted to violence only after the theft of one of their women? Did they murder each other and betray one another to the white man? Well, they do nothing of the sort in Nordhoff and Hall's novel. In Beechey's account sexual passion is the immediate cause of tragedy. While unable to eliminate the theme of lust that plays so conspicuous a part in all the accounts of Pitcairn Island, Nordhoff and Hall relegate it to a subsidiary position. By placing the wooing of a native woman by one of the mutineers earlier in the story and the enslavement of the Polynesians much later, the authors attribute the revolt to a manly desire for freedom rather than to sexual jealousy. Furthermore, when the native men do rebel in *Pitcairn's Island*, they fight with less duplicity than they display in Beechey's account. In the latter, for example, Tetahiti lures McCoy into an ambush; in Nordhoff and Hall's book he is a much more forthright fighter.

The Polynesians are not the only ones whose conduct Nordhoff and Hall tidy up. Beechey relates that Alexander Smith, the only mutineer remaining alive when the *Topaz* arrived at the island and the one who converted all the inhabitants to Christianity, scampered off into the woods for safety as soon as the natives went on a rampage. In *Pitcairn's Island*, however, he heroically sets out to warn Christian.

As novelists, Nordhoff and Hall were under no obligation to adhere rigidly to Beechey's version. The two writers had several alternative and, in many ways, conflicting reports from which they could draw. To be sure, all of the accounts were derived directly or indirectly from one source, Alexander Smith. But either Smith had a very capricious memory, or some of his auditors misconstrued what they heard. In one version, for instance, Christian, after the death of his wife, forcibly takes the wife of one of the Polynesians; in the other versions it is Williams who does so.[16] According to Captain Folger of the *Topaz*, Smith placed the suicide of McCoy before the rebellion of the native men, whereas, in Beechey's account, the event occurs much later. Folger's version also differs from Beechey's in that, in the former, only one mutineer, Smith, survives the native uprising; Beechey, however, asserts that McCoy, Quintal, and Young escaped too.[17] There are dozens of such discrepancies. The task of unraveling this skein of contradictions is too formidable to undertake in this study, which, after all, is concerned not primarily with the actual events on Pitcairn but with Hall's and his partner's handling of these events. Suffice it to say that, with so many conflicting versions to choose from, Nordhoff and Hall had nearly as much latitude in selecting and ordering incidents and in shaping characters as they would have had if they had been writing pure fiction.

However, if the defects of the Polynesians are mitigated in *Pitcairn's Island*, those defects are taken into account more than is usually the case in Hall's works. The white men may precipitate the tragedy, but, when the natives retaliate, they run amok, slaughtering and mutilating their oppressors with a fury far removed from the gentleness of the amiable hedonists who cavort through the pages of Hall's chapters in *Faery Lands of the South Seas*. Christian may be reflecting Hall's primitivism when he asserts that the Polynesians are "fine fellows with one or perhaps two exceptions."[18] But fine fellows or not, the Polynesians lose our sympathy (something that rarely happens in Hall's writings) when they brutally set out to slaughter all the whites, even the good ones like Christian, Young, and Smith.

But, although white aggressiveness provokes the Polynesians in *Pitcairn's Island* to go on a savage rampage, paradise is not lost but only temporarily misplaced. After the carnage, Alexander Smith, the native women, and the children of mixed parentage rediscover it. But what a fragile little paradise it is! An isolated kindergarten presided over by a Bible-reading patriarch, it is an Eden without adult males except for the virtuous and elderly Smith and, hence, an Eden without sex. When a ship from the outside world finally intrudes, Smith says: "I do believe ye might search the world around without finding children more truly innocent and pure-minded than these" (327). The epilogue, however, implies that their innocence will not last long. Having learned of the civilized world through contact with the *Topaz*, one of the boys tells Smith: "But we want to know. All of us do! Why have you never told us of the other lands?" (332). Once more Hall and his collaborator are blaming Western civilization for the demise of a South Sea paradise. Yet surely the intrusion of an American vessel was not needed to bring tribulations to those children: puberty alone would have sufficed. But to make such an admission is to precede the possibility of paradise, white or Polynesian, Christian or pagan—in a world of adults. Rather than wrestle with such a dilemma, Hall and Nordhoff simply evade the problem.

The evasion, like similar ones throughout *Pitcairn's Island*, prevents the book from being told in the "robust, bloody, and slightly pornographic Elizabethan fashion" Nordhoff thought appropriate for the material. Perhaps his realization that the 1930s public would have rejected such a book made him consign to his partner the most violent scenes, the killing and drinking episodes, which the manuscript in the Grinnell College Library reveals to be Hall's work. But, even if such pressure had not existed, it is unlikely that Nordhoff, the author of such lightweight fare as *The Blue Lagoon* and *The Fledgling*, working alone could have produced a successful novel of the kind he envisioned. And it is inconceivable that Hall, given his temperament and values, could have contributed to the writing of it. In fact, in view of their divergent attitudes toward their inharmonious subject matter, *Pitcairn's Island* is probably the best work they could have contrived about the terrible events on Pitcairn. No one, after all, could reasonably expect that almost perfect fusion of talents which had made *Mutiny on the Bounty* so extraordinary to have occurred often. The remarkable thing is that it occurred even a few times. In writing *Pitcairn's*

Island, Nordhoff and Hall came close enough to achieving it to produce an engrossing novel but not close enough to contain completely the centrifugal forces that beset the unity of the book.

III   *Hall's* Bounty *Postscript*

When an opportunity arose to visit Pitcairn Island after the completion of the *Bounty* trilogy, Hall seized it promptly. Nordhoff, however, who did not share his friend's enthusiasm for travel, remained behind in Tahiti. *The Tale of a Shipwreck* is Hall's account of the trip. The main theme, though, is not Pitcairn but life in the South Seas as a healthy mean between a frenzied existence in the Western world and the total solitude that persistently beckoned to Hall like a siren.

The opening pages offer a résumé of Hall's boyhood longing to go to the South Pacific, his wartime adventures, his purchase of Sir John Barrow's book about the *Bounty* in Paris, and the growth of his friendship with Nordhoff. He then describes the outward voyage of the *Pro Patria*, his sojourn on Pitcairn, the wrecking of the schooner on the reef of tiny Timoe Island, his stay first on Timoe and later on the larger nearby island of Mangareva, and finally his return to Tahiti in a cutter.

This slender narrative line is festooned with Hall's reflections on Bligh and Christian, New York and Pitcairn, Iowa and Polynesia, books and people, friendship and loneliness, and dozens of other matters little and great. Yet it all coheres, as Hall's autobiographical writing generally does, because he is able to make past and present illuminate each other and to make his comments, in turn, illuminate both. One characteristic episode begins with a description of Hall sitting aboard his schooner as it sails across the lagoon of Mangareva in the Tuamotu Archipelago.[19] The experience makes him recall works by Stevenson and Conrad. Soon, through a chain of associations, his thoughts wend back, as they were so often to do, to his boyhood in Iowa. We should note, however, that into this short passage he injects a reference to the First World War. This reference, in turn, prepares for his discussion a couple paragraphs later of Fletcher Christian because, as we have seen, it was from Barrow's book, purchased in Paris during the war, that Hall first learned the details of the *Bounty*'s story. And so on he goes, building up his narrative and at the same time garnishing it with exposition in his own inimitable and, alas, indescribable manner. The effect is leisurely. It is also charming and often amusing. But it is never chaotic or frivolous.

Despite its amiable tone, *The Tale of a Shipwreck* contains some of Hall's sharpest criticisms of life in postwar America. The gist of these criticisms is that the United States had been taken over by an "army of Babbitts" serving "the twin-headed god, Business and Science" (11). The entire country, as a result, seemed so feverish with pointless activity that Hall, in reaction, yearned for tranquility. Furthermore, conditions after the Treaty of Versailles made the entire Western world seem awash in "meddle and muddle." Thus he had sought refuge in the South Seas, which since Captain Cook's days had epitomized for many Europeans and Americans simplicity and serenity.

Hall informs us that he also craved privacy and even, at times, total solitude partly in response to the way technological growth was making the earth seem smaller and hence more crowded. His memory, too, of barrack life during the war intensified his urge to be alone "on some uninhabited island in the farthermost seas" (6). Yet, despite his desire to live apart, Hall concedes that he has only occasionally doubted the truth of George Santayana's contention that man is rooted in society. The dream of living alone, though, has continued to entice him.

Lest anyone wonder what all this has to do with the *Bounty* and Pitcairn Island, we must point out that in *The Tale of a Shipwreck* Hall's reflections on the mutiny and its aftermath function as motifs that harmonize with the account of his quest for solitude. For Hall Pitcairn seems less the locale of horrendous events than the apotheosis of isolation. There he finds a mode of life which confirms his antipathy toward the large concentrations of people in Western nations. Of the islanders he contends: "Whenever I meet such people I become increasingly convinced that mankind should breed less prolifically, and gather in less antlike heaps" (47).

Now, of course, these comments make Hall sound like an early advocate of zero population growth. But they also once more show him to be admiring in a distant land, as he had done in the Tuamotus and Iceland, those qualities of his native Colfax that he believed had been destroyed by the automobile and other technological scourges. And, as he wanders about Adamstown, the tiny capital of Pitcairn, he is reminded not of Iowa, to be sure—the mountainous terrain and the shantylike dwellings preclude such an association—but of settlements in western Virginia and eastern

Tennessee, which shared Colfax's smallness and isolation.

As for Pitcairn's most famous inhabitant, Fletcher Christian, when Hall directs his thoughts toward him he comes to seem more like a South Pacific Thoreau than like the guilt-ridden hero of Byron's *The Island*. In fact, in his strolls about Pitcairn, Hall becomes convinced that the mate of the *Bounty* must have had his happy moments there because "a man exiled for life to a lonely island . . . is not wholly to be pitied, granted that he has the resources within himself" (56). Hall's further comments on the matter leave little doubt that he felt Christian had possessed such resources.

The book leaves even less doubt that Hall found Christian a more sympathetic figure than he found Bligh. After acknowledging the captain's merits, Hall concludes that Bligh "had only himself to blame for the melancholy outcome of the breadfruit voyage" (128). Christian, on the other hand, Hall praises for being a "man of good birth, breeding and education—a brave, fiery spirited, and thoroughly competent officer." Christian's only sin, Hall seems to feel, was his inability to "endure in silence the outbursts of un-merited abuse" which Bligh heaped upon him (29). Hall's bias is so strongly in Christian's favor, in fact, that we must wonder how he could have contributed to the adulatory view of Bligh which pervades *Men Against the Sea*.

The explanation perhaps lies in the pages of *The Tale of a Shipwreck*. When, after the destruction of the *Pro Patria*, Hall is in an open boat, he identifies himself if not with Bligh then with the men in the *Bounty*'s launch under Bligh's command. Of the captain's exploits after the mutineers had cast him adrift, Hall writes: "There he was superb—one man in a thousand" (128).

In truth, the theme which unifies the diverse strands of *The Tale of a Shipwreck* is that people are at their most attractive when bound together in small bands whether as castaways in a boat or as inhabitants of a tiny inaccessible island. Obviously he finds them least appealing in large concentrations. But whether he believes prolonged individual isolation potentially beneficial remains the book's great unanswered question. Throughout his journey to Pitcairn he thinks it *might* be, and he keeps insisting that he would like to experiment with living completely alone for a long period of time. But, when the opportunity to perform the experiment finally arises on Timoe Island, he decides that he must return to his family in Tahiti. He assures himself, however, that "the experiment is only postponed and that someday . . ." (118). But the sentence trails off, unresolved. And, back at last in Tahiti, he proclaims: "I realized more clearly than ever before how deep was the affection I felt for this tropical little island" (120). Thus Tahiti emerges as a larger Pitcairn or as an immobile open boat—a place where pleasant people form an isolated band. As such, it is an agreeable mean between the teeming bustle of Europe and America and the perhaps dangerous enticements of individual solitude.

Hall, to be sure, had dealt with most of these matters in earlier works. His flight from the turmoil of postwar life in the Western world and his yearning for privacy had been major themes in his chapters of *Faery Lands of the South Seas*. And there, as well as in various selections in *On the Stream of Travel* and *Mid-Pacific*, he had at least touched upon nearly all the subjects treated in *The Tale of a Shipwreck*. Never before, however, had he handled them at such length. This entertaining yet provocative book demonstrates that in 1934 Hall, working without his partner, could still extract valuable ore from the veins he had mined so assiduously throughout the 1920s.

CHAPTER 7

Three More With and One Without Nordhoff

I   The Hurricane

I F *The Tale of a Shipwreck* demonstrated that Hall could work even better than before alone, *The Hurricane* (1936) revealed that he could work as well as ever with Nordhoff. Using the same method of composition they had employed in writing *Falcons of France* and the *Bounty* trilogy, the team produced a book which initially rivaled *Mutiny on the Bounty* in popularity and perhaps surpassed it in the enthusiasm it elicited from reviewers. Writers in the London *Times* and the *Yale Review* praised it lavishly, and Lewis Garnett in the *New York Herald Tribune* went so far as to compare it with the achievements of Robert Louis Stevenson and Joseph Conrad. Among critics in major publications, only Otis Ferguson in the *New Republic* struck a disharmonious chord when he declared that the work fell short of the tragedy to which it pretended, but even he commended the evocative powers of its authors.[1]

That *The Hurricane* is brilliantly evocative no one is likely to deny. Ferguson erred, however, in accusing Nordhoff and Hall of aspiring to tragedy. Like its predecessors, *The Hurricane* is overtly melodramatic. But, as in *Mutiny on the Bounty*, the authors used the apparatus of melodrama to move and instruct their reader as well as to divert him. The work, in fact, is quite successful in its own terms. If it is less powerful than *Mutiny on the Bounty*, the explanation is that it does not have that solid foundation in momentous historical events which Nordhoff and Hall had employed to impart a sense of importance as well as of verisimilitude to their earlier novel.

This is not to say that *The Hurricane* is unrealistic or that it does not deal with matters of significance. But, whereas in *Mutiny on the*

90

Bounty they had converted history into myth without destroying a sense of actuality, in writing *The Hurricane* Nordhoff and Hall fabricated a kind of extended parable which exposes the more oppressive features of European rule in the South Pacific and denounces that old bugaboo of theirs, pedantic authoritarianism. True, they embellished their tale with marvelously vivid descriptions of the South Seas. But an aura of artifice at times emanates from the work, as so often happens with didactic fiction.

By and large, however, the work is absorbing and convincingly makes its points. The plot gets under way when Terangi, the noble scion of warrior chiefs of Manukura Island in the Tuamotu Archipelago, strikes a bigoted white man who calls him a "nigger." (The bigot, with apposite irony, turns out to be a visiting Laborite politician.) Imprisoned in Tahiti, Terangi refuses to submit to incarceration even for the six months to which he has been sentenced. Escape follows escape, and his term is extended to five years. Undeterred, he tries once more, but this time he accidentally kills a guard. The white man's laws, though, make no allowance for such accidents, and so Terangi is to be transferred to the penal colony in French Guiana.

To be sure, as Nordhoff and Hall narrate these incidents, they sometimes oversimplify their dichotomy between noble native and nasty white man. But after allowance is made for the dictates of didacticism, the events are all too believable. White men have not been the most tolerant of people; a high-spirited Polynesian chief is not likely to be fond of prison life; and a man who consistently breaks jail is apt to convert a short sentence into a long one. Furthermore, these occurrences are related in a few pages where their main purpose is to create sympathy for Terangi, who is to remain a fugitive throughout most of the remainder of the novel; hence the need for simplification.

After the last of his escapes in Tahiti, Terangi makes his way back to his native island. There he finds his faithful young wife, Marama; a kindly old priest, Father Paul, who helps him; and an assortment of admirable natives. He also encounters a pedantic governor, de Laage, who hunts him, and the governor's sympathetic wife, who pleads for him. Of these characters de Laage is the most interesting. He is a man to whom small things are as important as large ones, "a man of unalterable habit, scrupulously exact in performing all the little routine duties of life."[2]

De Laage is something of a caricature, more ludicrous than terrible. But this fact in no respect diminishes his effectiveness in the book and may even enhance it. Nordhoff and Hall recognized, as Charles Dickens did, that when the plot manipulations and happy endings of comedy are combined with the serious subject matter and tone of tragedy to produce what is often termed melodrama, certain methods of characterization and development which would vitiate tragedy can vitalize this kind of hybrid work.

Thus we do not groan when the climactic event of the book, the great hurricane, becomes a device for righting wrongs and resolving conflicts. The hurricane has to do something important enough to justify the preparations Nordhoff and Hall have made for it throughout the novel. Yet it cannot kill Terangi and Marama: if they are not too good to be true, they are too good to die a death so irrelevant to the work's main theme, the need to temper law with mercy. De Laage, on the other hand, is too bad to be allowed to live on with his prejudices intact but ridiculous enough with his pedantic legalisms to be granted the comic villain's reprieve of a last-minute conversion before he perishes of fever in Guiana, offstage in the same epilogue in which Terangi is granted the inevitable pardon.

But if such contrivances will not ruin a book of this sort, a lack of vividness will. We can accept a degree of artificiality in plot and characterization in *The Hurricane* (as, once again, we accept it in Dickens's novels) because the setting is so lifelike that it confers credibility upon the people and the incidents in the work. In view of the close cooperation between the two authors, we must credit both men for this merit of the novel as for any other it possesses. Yet the indisputable fact is that most of the book's action occurs in a portion of the Pacific with which Hall had been identified much more intimately than had Nordhoff—the Tuamotu Archipelago. Unlike Nordhoff, who was loath to travel, Hall had visited the island group often and had written about it with affection many times, first in his chapters in *Faery Lands of The South Seas* back in 1921 and most recently in *The Tale of a Shipwreck* a mere two years earlier. Loving solitude as he did, Hall discovered an austere loveliness in those remote, sun-baked specks of land. Because of what he had done for atolls in *Faery Lands of the South Seas* and in numerous subsequent works, we must assume that the major impetus to depict it so knowingly and enthusiastically came from Hall.

Another feature of *The Hurricane* which bears Hall's imprint is the character of Dr. Kersaint, who narrates much of the story.

Perhaps because Kersaint functions principally as an observer and does not have to conform to the convolutions of the plot, he seems a more fully integrated character than Roger Byam in *Mutiny on the Bounty* does. He also is more like Hall than like Nordhoff. Remote, lonely places appeal to him for the same reason they appealed to Hall—because they are far removed from "the world of our times." He has sought refuge in isolated spots such as the Tuamotu Archipelago because the world in which his "youth was passed was in ruins" (10 - 11). "When I first came to Manukura," he says, "I could never have enough of solitude" (130). And, in so saying, he echoes dozens of similar statements in Hall's essays. When he explains his love of poetry, Kersaint sums up the theme of an article Hall had written back in 1916:[3] "During the war it was my unfailing consolation in a world gone mad save for the poets" (130 - 31). Kersaint also shares Hall's enthusiasm for the Polynesians' propensity for living in the present "without forethought" and Hall's admiration for their lack of "greed, parsimony, avarice" (34,15). He confesses his own want of ambition, scoffs at progress, and insists that, despite the class distinctions among them, "Polynesians are the most democratic of people" (14-15, 76).

Kersaint, in short, seems to be virtually Hall's alter ego. Yet, if the narrator is pure Hall, the story, with its impulsive hero fighting bravely and unreflectingly for freedom against civilized injustice and legal pedantry, is pure Nordhoff. Terangi is no beach-lolling Pan; he is the two-fisted kind of hero Nordhoff had celebrated in his portion of *Faery Lands of the South Seas*. He beats up bullies, aids women in distress, and, when the hurricane strikes, he is ready to take command. After he receives his pardon he becomes not an atoll philosopher but a vigorous ship's captain.

Now, it may seem that such an action-filled story would not lend itself to being narrated by a seeker of solitude and a lover of tranquility. But, as a matter of fact, story and storyteller here complement each other admirably. Kersaint, introspective, detached, and, at the same time, sympathetic, helps mute the melodrama of *The Hurricane*. Furthermore, he accomplishes what a more brusque, matter-of-fact narrator could never achieve—he describes with sensitivity the atoll itself and the storm that pummels it. So effective, in fact, is this fusion of a Hall-like narrator with a Nordhoff-like tale that only its more restricted scope and its slightly greater aura of contrivance prevent *The Hurricane* from being the full equal of *Mutiny on the Bounty*.

II   The Dark River

The Hurricane, one of Nordhoff and Hall's best efforts, was
followed two years later (1938) by one of their worst, *The Dark
River*. So unsatisfactory is it that even Paul L. Briand, Jr., who
usually finds something favorable to say about the writings of
Nordhoff and / or Hall, concedes that the novel is a failure.[4]
   It is tempting to blame the defects of the work upon the marital
difficulties which beset Nordhoff after the completion of *The
Hurricane*. His domestic problems, after all, were soon to culminate
in a divorce that left him embittered and that precipitated the
prolonged decline from which he never wholly recovered. But such
an explanation will not suffice. Undoubtedly, to produce works of
the caliber of *Mutiny on the Bounty* and *The Hurricane*, both
authors needed to function at the topmost level of their talents.
Never again were they to reach that level. Of the four remaining
books they were to write together, however, two—*No More Gas*
(1940) and *Botany Bay* (1941)—are considerably better than ade-
quate.
   Perhaps Nordhoff and Hall erred this time in really attempting
tragedy, a mode unsuited to their temperaments both as a team and
as individuals. The fact is that in this work they reverse their usual
pattern, which is to give an unhappy course of events a happy ending. *The Dark River* throughout promises a smile-evoking resolution
that never comes. The book, in fact, opens with one of the hoariest
ploys of comedy, the concealed-identity device. Naia believes
herself to be the daughter of Mauri, a Tahitian widow, but is actually the child of a deceased English couple, the McLeods. It seems
that Mauri, whose own daughter was stillborn, saw no harm in ap-
propriating the newborn infant of Mrs. McLeod when its mother
died. Now, who should suddenly appear in Tahiti eighteen or so
years later but George McLeod, Naia's real brother. With him is
another young Englishman, Alan Hardie. Alan loses no time in falling in love with Naia, but there is a complication: his father,
General Hardie, is a good old soul who has a regrettable prejudice
against nonwhites. True, Naia is as white as a Ku Klux Klan mask,
but she does not know she is, and neither do Alan and George.
Nobody knows, in fact, except Mauri, who is not going to reveal the
truth because she will disgrace herself before her neighbors and lose
Naia, whom she loves.
   If there was ever a situation right out of eighteenth-century farce

or Gilbert and Sullivan comic opera, this is it. It is true that other important American authors have dealt with miscegenation and other racial problems in terms of white characters who are mistakenly presumed to be nonwhite or who have only an infinitesimal amount of nonwhite blood. Twain in *Pudd'nhead Wilson*, Faulkner in *Absalom, Absalom!* and *Light in August*, Sinclair Lewis in *Kingsblood Royal*, and George Washington Cable in stories like "Tite Poulette" and "Madame Dauphine" come readily to mind. In the best of these works, however, the truth, when it becomes known, can bring only tragedy or pathos: and the revelation of that truth is skillfully foreshadowed.

In *The Dark River*, on the other hand, the revelation does not come. Mauri keeps finding excuses for remaining silent; Alan and Naia elope to the Tuamotu coral islands, where they are shipwrecked on one of the most remote atolls of the archipelago. After two years of bliss, they return to Tahiti. But Alan has gone blind. One day, General Hardie arrives. True, he wants no coffee-colored children in *his* family, but his son is his son, and a father does have his duties. From his father, Alan learns that, blind or not, he can return to England and resume his astronomical work at Oxford. The native wife, of course, will have to be left in Tahiti. Well, Alan is no bounder; astronomy is all very fine, but love comes first. In the midst of this plot impasse, Naia recalls an old Tahitian remedy for blindness. Everything appears ready for a comic-opera climax and a happy denouement. Naia will cure Alan's blindness, and his grateful father will overcome his racial prejudice and acknowledge his daughter-in-law. All three will sail off to England, but not before Mauri has revealed the true parentage of Naia. But Nordhoff and Hall provide another climax. Naia, while plucking from a cliffside flowers needed for her Polynesian remedy for Alan's blindness, loses her footing and plummets to her death. After her funeral, Alan, in despair, kills himself. General Hardie belatedly discovers from Mauri the true parentage of his late daughter-in-law, and, filled with remorse, he embarks for England with Alan's son.

The saddest thing about *The Dark River* is not the fate of its principal characters but that lost within its tangled plot are elements of authentic tragedy. It has an important theme—racial prejudice. It has, in General Hardie, a character whose pride leads to the destruction of the son he loves. There is in Hardie's plight, moreover, genuine irony. Faithful to the code of his milieu and desiring only the happiness of his son, he brings misery to both his

son and himself. Too little, however, is done with Hardie; Nordhoff
and Hall permit him to remain a peripheral ogre—well-meaning,
but ponderous and obtuse. By putting the emphasis on the insipid
young lovers and by relying heavily on surprising incidents, the
authors produced in *The Dark River* a kind of Book-of-the-Month
Club *Romeo and Juliet*—that is, a *Romeo and Juliet* without poetry
and without the aura of inexorable doom indispensable to tragedy.

The best feature of *The Dark River* is its descriptions of Tahiti
and the Tuamotu Archipelago. The reader of today is likely to agree
with Elmer Davis, who, writing in 1938, dismissed the book's
significance as a novel but found it effective as a travelogue that
"makes anybody in a disheartened pre-war world feel like getting
away from it all while there is still time."[5] "Pre-war" only need be
changed to "post-war" to make the statement still applicable. Yet,
although *The Dark River* effectively evokes the charm of atoll life,
there are sturdier literary vessels for anyone who wishes to voyage
vicariously to Polynesian low islands—not the least among them being Hall's sketches and, of course, his chapters in *Faery Lands of
the South Seas*.

III   No More Gas

The next book Nordhoff and Hall produced, their only comedy,
deals with an improvident half-caste Tahitian family, the Tuttles.
Actually, both the tone of *No More Gas*, an amused affection for
Polynesian fiscal irresponsibility, and the basic pattern of its action
were anticipated in a story Nordhoff wrote back in 1927, "Maki's
Perfect Day."[6] The principal attraction of the book, however, is
neither its tone nor story line, although many of the incidents are
amusing, but rather its central character, Jonas Tuttle, who is
something of a South Sea Mr. Micawber with elements of Walter
Mitty and a dash of James Norman Hall as he depicts himself in
"Sing: A Song of Sixpence." Jonas, with the eager assistance of
other members of the Tuttle clan, of which he is the head, has
squandered the patrimony originally bequeathed by a New
England-born ancestor. No debt is ever too great to deter him from
giving a lavish party, no financial setback severe enough to dispel
for long his incorrigible optimism. Kept solvent almost solely by the
generosity of Dr. Blondin, he lolls about, dreaming of sending a
check to Montgomery Ward and Company for $4982.54 with which

he hopes to purchase "wanted articles ranging from wind-mills to mouth organs."[7] Virtually impecunious, he rents a Lincoln automobile from a Papeete garage; and, while riding in it, he can easily imagine that the vehicle, its horn, and its driver all belong to him. He lives, in fact, in a world of delightful fairy tales which become, at least for the moment, utterly real to him. Unfortunately, reality keeps intruding; demands are made for payments of debts. His benefactor, Dr. Blondin, yielding to the urgings of a lawyer, ceases to lend money indiscriminately and forces Jonas to sign papers promising to repay the loans in installments. When the Tuttle family, through sheer luck, comes into a fortune—some of the boys salvage an abandoned ship—Jonas squanders it all in a few months, loses the sum he has set aside to repay Dr. Blondin, and gets the entire clan evicted from their estate. Of course, everything ends well for him: he finds the lost money, makes the payment, recovers his property. But, at the conclusion of the book, he remains unreformed and unreformable.

Few books probably have been less intended for ponderous analysis: fewer still have less needed it. Even without the explanatory remarks Nordhoff and Hall provide, it would be obvious that Jonas and his clan represent the joyous hedonism and delightful impracticality of the Polynesians in a world becoming increasingly devoted to commerce. The Tuttles live for the present. Such irresponsibility, of course, is a perpetual source of annoyance to industrious white men like the lawyer Dorme. Convinced that the Tuttles need a lesson, he says to the generous Dr. Blondin: "You've demoralized them with your easy-going ways in this matter" (105 - 106). Nordhoff and Hall leave little doubt where their sympathies lie. They favor, of course, not the Mr. Dormes of this world but the Tuttles and men who humor them like Dr. Blondin.

One criticism could be made of *No More Gas*—that its comedy is directed principally not at the people of whom we are supposed to disapprove, the Dormes, but at the lovable Tuttles. As a result Tahitian values emerge as quaint and absurd. We may *like* the Tuttles; but, since only the most incredible good fortune saves them from ruin, the novel does little to make us want to emulate them. Yet in the giddy comic world of *No More Gas*, the rescue of the Tuttles seems as inevitable as the downfall of Oedipus does in Sophocles's play. Tahiti here is not the great world writ small but a rebuke to that world. People like the Tuttles should flourish everywhere—and would, if all the earth had the good sense to become like Nordhoff and Hall's South Sea island.

IV   The Friends: *A Volume in Verse*

In 1939 Hall published his first volume of poetry, a thirty-four-page blank-verse account of a colloquy between three men about Edward Arlington Robinson's verse. It seems odd that Hall should have waited until his fifty-second year to produce a book in the form that was dearest to him. After all, as a boy in Colfax he had been a woodshed poet; he had made his first debut as a writer with short verses printed in periodicals during his years as a social worker in Boston; and throughout his career his poems had appeared in various magazines.

Perhaps he recognized that he was seldom at his best in his poetry. To be sure, his verses, as Ellery Sedgwick has noted, are pleasant in an old-fashioned way.[8] But they lack the colloquial vigor that keeps his prose from seeming anachronistic. *The Friends,* however, sounds more contemporary than his poems generally do. One reason is that he used blank verse in it rather than the rhymes he usually favored. Another is that it is in dialogue form. Much of the work, in fact, reads like metrical prose which is more appropriate to the character of *The Friends* than a more "poetic" syntax and diction would be.

The conversation of the three friends grows out of a remark by one of them, a New Englander named Mills Waters, that people from other parts of the country cannot really understand Robinson's poems. Raleigh, a Virginian, ironically admits Waters may be right, then launches into a good-natured criticism of New England's parochialism, cultural pretentiousness, and, of course, its climate. But he proceeds to say that, despite some misgivings, he reads Robinson for the following reasons:

> Because I like a poet who remembers
> With deep respect, the soil from which he sprung.
> Because I like a poet who remembers
> That he is not phenomenal; with roots
> That deeply thrust into the soil that nourished poets
> Before his time.[9]

Raleigh here patently speaks for Hall. Elsewhere, however, a third friend, Crabbe, seems closer to the author's sentiments, especially when Crabbe states a preference for some of Robinson's shorter works over the longer Arthurian pieces and a fondness for the poet when he is most simple and straightforward.

It is Raleigh, however, who near the end seems to sum up Hall's attitude toward Robinson when he reads aloud a sonnet of his own in praise of the poet. At the very end, though, Waters still will not admit that non-New Englanders can fully understand Robinson, although he admits that Raleigh's poem "ain't so bad." And so, as Crabbe says, they are back where they started.

The Friends, in effect, is part literary criticism, part jest, part doggerel, part genuine poetry, and all Hall. Here are his oft-stated love of tradition, of writers with cultural roots, and his equally oft-enunciated antipathy toward quirky modernism, pretentiousness, and precipitous change. Here too are his humor, his sense of *bonhomie*, and his propensity for joking about literature while taking it seriously. It would be too pompous and too easy to berate the work for not being what it never pretends to be. A more reasonable response would be to delight in what it is—agreeable, literate, and intelligent.

CHAPTER 8

The Early Years of World War II

A S they move past fifty, many authors become less prolific. But Hall was not one of those authors. Whereas in the
1920s he had produced only four books, two with Nordhoff and two
without him, from 1939 (his fifty-second year) through 1945 he
wrote nine volumes, five without a coauthor. Moreover, because of
Nordhoff's waning powers even the jointly written work represented more of Hall's labors than of Nordhoff's.

Although these were good years for Hall, he was saddened by the
deterioration of Nordhoff as well as by the war engulfing the world.
Three of his books, in fact, deal directly with the conflict—*Men
Without Country, Lost Island,* and *The High Barbaree*—and portions of a fourth, *Under a Thatched Roof,* pertain to it. As we shall
see, the war sorely tested some of Hall's most cherished beliefs. Its
eventual impact upon his own beloved South Pacific, furthermore,
made him more than a detached spectator.

The first five books to appear during the war years, however, os-
tensibly have nothing to do with contemporary horrors. *The Friends*
and *No More Gas,* both of which we have examined, deal respectively with the poems of Edwin Arlington Robinson and with a
shiftless, lovable Tahitian family. The other three are set in the past.
Two, *Doctor Dogbody's Leg* and *Botany Bay,* take place in the late
eighteenth and early nineteenth centuries. In the other, *Oh
Millersville!* Hall returns to the Iowa of his boyhood.

I An Eighteenth-Century Opus

Doctor Dogbody's Leg is difficult to categorize. Hall's first piece
of sustained fiction written without a collaborator, it is not so much
a novel as a set of episodes bound together by a narrative
framework in the manner of *The Canterbury Tales.* Yet the tales
here are more integrated with each other than those in Chaucer's

work are. Hall's book, moreover, operates in a strange realm between realism and fantasy.

Each of the ten chapters contains a tale told by Doctor Feadle Dogbody, a retired ship's physician, to his companions at Will Tunn's Cheerful Tortoise Inn in Portsmouth, England, after the Napoleonic Wars. Every time the group gathers, someone says something that prompts Dogbody to launch off on a new story about how he has lost his leg. Generally he slips in the subject of the amputation as an aside or injects it as an anticlimax. All along, meanwhile, his friends pretend never to have heard about how he has lost his limb. The stories themselves are discursive, mock-heroic tales. But, for all their extravagance, whenever he concludes one, some detail in it is confirmed either by a person present or by a verifying object Dogbody brings from his pocket.

In and out of the book weave famous personages. Benjamin Franklin once designs for Dogbody a lifelike artificial leg. Catherine the Great of Russia tries to seduce him. And because of her, he loses his leg when she orders him thrown from her sled to allay the hunger of pursuing wolves. Elsewhere, John Adams and Franklin debate topics such as free will and the future of the new American republic.

It is significant that Hall, despite his oft-proclaimed optimism, makes the pessimistic Adams the better prophet. When Franklin asserts that "in our Western world, the way is clear, or will be soon, for a new approach to human happiness," the rejoinder which Hall puts into Adams's mouth is all too telling when read from a twentieth-century vantage point: "I foresee a time when it [the American continent] will be covered with swarms of rats and locusts in the shape of men. . . . They will be so eaten up with greed as neither to think nor care for the welfare of their children's children. Money will be their god. They will plough all their grasslands under in their eagerness for money crops. Eventually, endless clouds of dust will fill the air over the prairies, and our forests . . . will be laid waste, and the lands where they stood, sterile and barren."[1]

In fact, this funny, whimsical book which celebrates masculine good fellowship has a serious undercurrent. The world that Hall evokes is that of Britain on the brink of the industrial revolution. And if he makes that world seem in retrospect appealing, he hardly depicts it as Paradise. In the course of the book, we learn that British ships were stocked with "beef" derived from cats and dogs. We learn too that the "English of those days were the greatest traf-

fickers in human flesh and bone" (185). And one of the more gripping stories concerns a shipload of slaves from Africa. We are given
a chilling view of the "inhuman penal laws of England" (29). We
are also reminded of the havoc wreaked upon the countryside by
the Enclosure Acts and of how, as a result: "Poverty, starvation, and
the unspeakable social conditions of our country in general compel
thousands to steal and die" (310). And when the master of a convict
ship speaks to a woman who is the victim of a lustful wealthy man's
false charges, he does not depict their homeland as a Utopia when
he says: "If all them was transported that should be transported,
there'd be more churches empty than prisons. There'd be not a
score left in the seats of Parliament" (325). How is it that Dogbody,
the teller of these horrendous tales, can suffuse a nostalgic glow
over an era whose faults he acknowledges so freely? Part of the explanation is that he always contrives happy endings for his stories.
But it is also because, sanguine soul that he is, he has mastered an
art that Hall himself had learned as a combat pilot in World War I:
to endure pain and ugliness without wallowing in them and to enjoy
to a maximum whatever pleasures that come his way. Furthermore,
although he is ready to assist each suffering person he meets,
Dogbody does not allow his sensitivity to other people's pain, any
more than Hall did, to poison his life by turning him into a mis-
anthrope or into what Albert Camus called a metaphysical rebel,
shaking his fist futilely at the cosmos.

Hall, then, does not depict eighteenth-century England as an
Eden. But he envisions it, as he perceived Iowa of the late
nineteenth century and the South Seas afterward, as stable enough
not to spawn new horrors so rapidly that one could neither com-
prehend nor contend with them. Like Hall in Tahiti, Dogbody in
his eighteenth-century world has mastered his environment,
transforming it with his "lies," which are really the artist's way of
enhancing reality. There, among men who have time for fellowship
and good stories, Dogbody can be at home. Perhaps he could have
been at home anywhere or any time. But Europe or America after
1940 would have taxed his powers sorely.

II   *From the Mouths of Babes*

How seriously should a hoax be taken? The answer, of course,
depends upon the hoax. The circumstances surrounding the

publication of *Oh Millersville!* as well as the nature of the work seem to militate against too solemn a response to the book. After all, why ponder over a volume of doggerel verses presented as the efforts of a little girl who lived in a turn-of-the-century Iowa town? The fact that Hall several years later chortled publicly in an article in the *Atlantic* over the success of his ruse should ward off anybody pompous enough to dissect these confections offered in jest.

Perhaps the biggest joke about all this, however, is that *Oh Millersville!* provides the most complete illumination of Hall's attitudes toward his boyhood home, Colfax, Iowa. Indeed, the picture here of the prairie town is far more extensive, more varied in mood, and more concrete in its depiction of good and bad features of such a community than are the early chapters in Hall's autobiography, fine as those chapters are.

Knowing that the poems are not the work of a preadolescent girl, Fern Gravel, but of a middle-aged man heightens our delight in them. The artlessness is then seen to be art; the naive tone becomes a *faux naïf* irony which inverts complaints about the town into compliments and compliments into complaints. Even the occasional misspellings become a part of the comic apparatus.

Fern, though, is an ambivalent persona for her creator. Her priggish horror of alcohol, her small-town pietism, her awe of the president of the local bank make some of her perceptions antithetical to those of the mature Hall and by no means identical to those of Hall as a child. We should recall that he was fond of hoboes and had a puckish strain in his character, whereas Fern is forbiddingly respectable and completely humorless. At other times, however, she clearly speaks for him, expressing yearnings and antipathies he certainly must have felt at a similar age and to some extent continued to feel as an adult. Fern, for instance, shares Hall's discomfort with mathematics and his enthusiasm for reading. She also has his longing to travel, as she indicates in the following lines from the opening poem, which are a representative specimen of her versification:

> Millersville, oh, Millersville!
> That is my home and I like it, but still
> I wish that once in a while I could go
> To cities like Omaha and St. Jo.
> You get tired of living in such a small town
> With so few streets for walking around.[2]

Now, if one thing has emerged from this study, it should be that Hall was no lover of cities. He was, however, a lifelong devotee of wandering, and his numerous writings make it clear that from childhood he regarded the horizon as an enticement. Yet throughout Fern's poems we find a restless dissatisfaction with prairie-village life that Hall, when speaking directly for himself, rarely confesses to but which as a bright, inquiring boy he must have experienced. This does not mean, though, that either at the time or in retrospect he lacked affection for his hometown—quite the contrary! Even Fern concludes her poem by insisting that she would not want to stay in any of those big places.

As we have seen, Hall's thoughts frequently reverted to Colfax, even though he continued to reside throughout most of his adult life in the South Seas. Oddly enough the genesis of this book lay in the fusion in a dream of these two seemingly irreconcilable places. According to his account, the physical features of Iowa and Tahiti became so mixed up as to be nearly indistinguishable. At one point a group of children sang an old song, "Green gravel, green gravel." But the words became changed to "Fern gravel, fern gravel," and among the group was a little girl he had known back home named Fern. When he asked her where she lived, emulating the Pacific islanders who had told white men they were from "Otaheiti," she said she was from "Omillersville"—the name being suggested by a town near Colfax called Mitchelville.[3]

It could be that this imaginative fusion of Iowa and Tahiti, along with the use of Fern Gravel as a persona, liberated his imagination and loosened his reticence. Be that as it may, in these verses he suffuses the scenes of his youth with a warm glow while at the same time peopling them with far more disagreeable incidents and individuals than was generally the case when he wrote about Iowa. Even nature here is by no means always benign because aside from interminable winters it menaces Fern and her neighbors with cyclones. As for the residents of Millersville, among them are a fair share of asses and misfits and at least one bona fide monster. There is a librarian who removes a book about Mormons from her shelves when she learns it contains passages about polygamy; there is grouchy old Mrs. Shellenberger, who prevents her son from marrying an organist. There is also a town drunkard who is kept supplied with alcohol by Fern's druggist uncle—much to her dismay because, unlike Hall, she shares her neighbors' prohibitionist sentiments. On a more terrible level there is Mitchner, a hard-working, sadistic German who cuts his son's ears with shears.

But *Oh Millersville!* is anything but a catalogue of horrors. It is not even one of those broadside assaults on small-town dullness and provinciality which Midwestern writers have been inclined to write. Yes, Fern is sometimes bored, the long winters sometimes depress her, and some of her neighbors are objectionable. In the main, however, the people around her are well-meaning and generous. They take her on buggy rides and on train trips to other communities. And life in Millersville is enlivened by medicine shows, pianoplaying, reading, and sleigh-riding. Indeed, for all her vexation with the rigors of the cold months, she says in one poem, "Winter Music," that she could not endure living in a land "without a bobsled or a sleigh" (69)—a fine remark from the mouthpiece of a resident of Tahiti!

Ultimately, what gives *Oh Millersville!* its value is not its success as a hoax. Neither is it the nostalgia which suffuses many of its verses. It is, rather, the wide-ranging and balanced perception which Hall provides of turn-of-the-century rural Iowa. The fact that he takes greater cognizance of the defects of that vanished world than he was usually to present in his writings paradoxically makes his account more poignant. Utopias, by their very nature, are incredible. But Fern Gravel's milieu, with its sprinkling of dolts and neurotics, its petty vexations and occasional disasters, is real enough for us to believe in and appealing enough, despite its imperfections, for us to mourn its passing as James Norman Hall, the wielder of Fern's pen, mourned it.

III   *Social Corruption*

Nordhoff seems to have been a reluctant contributor to the next book to bear his name. In fact, throughout these years ill health and personal problems made writing of any kind often at best onerous and sometimes literally impossible for him. In spite of his antipathy toward travel, however, he allowed Hall to persuade him to go to Australia to collect data for their new novel, which was to be about the penal colony there. Instead of finding the trip stimulating, as they had both hoped he would, he was more depressed in Sydney than he had been in Tahiti. When he returned home, he all but abandoned the project to Hall, who forthwith set to work converting Nordhoff's findings into fiction. Nordhoff, however, later decided to assist Hall, partly because an enticing offer had come from Hollywood.

If *Botany Bay* makes extensive use of Nordhoff's gleanings from his Australian excursion, it also utilizes Hall's ruminations about eighteenth-century England, which he had exploited so effectively in *Doctor Dogbody's Leg*. But, whereas *Doctor Dogbody's Leg* often celebrates the Britain of that period while conceding its defects, *Botany Bay* reverses the process. In the latter book England emerges as a disagreeable place with a few redeeming virtues. The novel, in fact, provides a Dickensian panorama of the social, political, and economic inequities of that era.

The hero, Hugh Tallant, is an American Loyalist who fights for England during the Revolutionary War and then flees from his home in Maryland first to Nova Scotia and thence to London. Instead of being rewarded for his loyalty to the Crown, he finds himself destitute. So desperate does he become that he joins forces with Tom Oakley, an amiable highwayman.

After he and Oakley are apprehended, nothing he sees about the penal system increases his esteem for England. Conditions in Newgate Prison are deplorable. The inmates live in unspeakable squalor unless they are rich enough to bribe the corrupt officials. As for the guards, they are a coarse, brutal lot. Indeed, the only decent people he meets there are fellow criminals—among them a Falstaffian fence named Nick Sabb, a personable pickpocket, and a cultivated family, the Thynnes, whose members specialize in burglarizing homes of the rich, into which they gain entry as partycrashers.

Needless to say, conditions aboard the ship which transports him to the new penal colony in Australia are far from idyllic. It is not surprising, therefore, that, when a fellow convict on the *Charlotte*—an American named Monro who is a dedicated revolutionist—asks Hugh whether he regrets having chosen the English side in the recent war, he replies promptly in the affirmative. After denouncing the British class system and announcing his determination to fight for the emancipation of Canada, Monro dies, leaving behind a daughter, Sally, to provide the novel with a love interest.

In Australia Hugh is hardly off the boat before he gets a graphic glimpse of the plight of the aborigines when a fellow convict kills an unoffending native. Although Governor Phillip is wise and just, Hugh soon resolves to escape. Following a frustrated attempt to flee in an American brig with Sally, who is carried off in it before her lover can join her, Hugh and his companions undertake an openboat voyage along the Australian coast reminiscent of Bligh's feat in the *Bounty's* launch. After all manner of ordeals, they are rescued by a Dutch vessel which carries them to England.

Back in London, Hugh again slides promptly into the ghastly underside of English life. Poverty, slums, and corrupt police officials are his daily lot until he encounters Sally and an old family friend, Mr. Fielding, who informs him that he has been pardoned and granted a ten-thousand pound compensation for his losses in the Revolutionary War. Now he and his sweetheart can marry. He has no desire, however, to return to Maryland with its painful memories. Evidently, though, some painful memories are less agonizing than others because he and Sally elect to return to Australia as free settlers.

But the novel does not end on this organ peal of affirmation. Hugh's old partner in highway banditry, Tom Oakley, has been arrested again, and this time it is to be the gallows for him. Now we find ourselves back in Newgate among scenes of Hogarthian degradation. Oakley's execution itself becomes a well-nigh apocalyptic event when the crowd panics and large numbers of spectators are trampled to death. In the epilogue Hugh, shortly before his departure for Australia, meets by chance the two spoiled, vain daughters of Mortimer Thynne, who is still a prisoner in Sydney. The book concludes with Hugh seated on a bench in Hyde Park watching the frivolous creatures walk off.

It should be readily apparent to anybody who has read *Mutiny on the Bounty* that a strong kinship exists between the two novels. In both, the action occurs principally in the late eighteenth century. Both also regale their readers with imprisonments, harsh punishments, last-minute rescues, maritime adventures, and idyllic pictures of primitive lands. In both, too, the story is narrated by an old man who has chosen to remain loyal to England even though he has suffered grievous wrongs at its hands and who has since been rewarded for that loyalty with a long and prosperous life.

The differences between the two works, however, are equally striking. For one thing, *Botany Bay* is far more bitter. In *Mutiny on the Bounty*, we see little of the nether side of eighteenth-century British life ashore. In *Botany Bay*, on the other hand, we see almost nothing else throughout the first four and the concluding five chapters. Furthermore most of the outrages in the earlier book occur under two captains (Bligh and Edwards) who are presented as being excessively severe even by the standards of their own time. The scenes of squalor and oppression in the slums and prisons of

Botany Bay, though, are patently intended to typify pervasive evils.

The indictment of this society is compounded by the fact that the protagonist, an upright young Tory, is driven to highway robbery by economic conditions. It should be recalled that Hugh's counterpart in *Mutiny on the Bounty*, Roger Byam, never even considers supporting the insurrection against the captain and that Byam could no more have become a common criminal than he could have become a snake charmer. Hugh Tallant not only turns to crime; he finds many criminals preferable to the authorities who arrest and punish them. Although the novel abounds in odious felons, the general impression Nordhoff and Hall convey in *Botany Bay* is that people imprisoned for breaking the law are as a group no worse than those who make and enforce the laws.

Botany Bay, however, is more than a condemnation of a bygone society. It is tantamount to a denunciation of Western industrial-commercial civilization itself. Even the pioneer spirit which animates Hugh is tarnished by the fact that he is an unwitting harbinger of the forces he flees Europe to escape from. In the novel's opening pages he reveals that he and Sally are abandoning their farm near Sydney because the country thereabouts has become as crowded and as "tame" as England. Moreover, the viciousness of the mob in Maryland that had burned down his family's home should have taught him that people in "new" worlds are apt to behave as badly as denizens of older ones. And Hugh makes it clear that he regards Australia as another America. But its brutal treatment of its aborigines certainly suggests that, if it has some of America's former promise, it is also repeating America's crimes and errors. That it should repeat them is hardly astonishing: both are the offspring of the same corrupt civilization.

Perhaps the bleakness of *Botany Bay* reflects Nordhoff's melancholy state of mind induced by his personal troubles and intensified by his disappointing trip to Australia. Perhaps it mirrors the growing apprehensions of both authors over the state of their war-wracked planet. Whatever the explanation, the book is one of the least optimistic they produced either as a team or as individuals.

Of course, the novel has its flickers of brightness: Hall's participation alone would have insured at least a glimmer of hope in its pages. If *Botany Bay* is awash with villainy, private and social, it contains many decent, generous, humane characters in all levels of society from Governor Phillip of Australia down to incorrigible criminals like Nick Sabb and Ned Inching. And amid all the horrors which befall him, Hugh never relinquishes his pastoral ideal which he finally attains in New South Wales, despite the encroachments of "civilization" toward the end of his long life. But, whereas in Hall's works ugly incidents rarely efface the overall idyllic effect, in this novel the suffering is too widespread, too prolonged, and too graphically depicted to be mitigated by its few brief lyrical descriptions of Australian or English landscapes.

Why then, with this somber treatment of a serious subject, is not *Botany Bay* a better book than *Mutiny on the Bounty?* The main reason is that its disparate elements are less effectively fused than are the strands in the earlier book. In *Mutiny on the Bounty* Nordhoff and Hall blended history, myth, melodrama, and realism to produce a wholly satisfying work. The problem with *Botany Bay* is that the importance of its subject matter, the frequent grimness of its tone, and the wide scope of its action seem incongruent with the conventions of adventure fiction which Nordhoff and Hall use to move along their story—reprieves, pardons, sudden rescues, chance meetings, timely demises, and the rest. To be sure, Dickens often makes such incongruities work. But he does it by creating a special world, real yet fantastic, as Nordhoff and Hall produced a special although a quite different world in *Mutiny on the Bounty*. In *Botany Bay*, where they to some extent trespass on Dickens's realm—prisons and slums populated with grotesque low-life types—they lack that steadiness of vision which had often sustained them when they had concentrated on the South Seas or the high seas. The book, consequently, sometimes seems less a fusing of reality and fantasy than a veering back and forth between them. Yet, despite that flaw, *Botany Bay* is gripping and memorable—an ambitious book that may not quite reach its objectives but that comes closer to attaining them than anyone has a reasonable right to expect.

CHAPTER 9

The World in Disarray

I A Sane Voice Above the Din

THROUGHOUT the 1930s and early 1940s Hall had not neglected his favorite prose genre, the essay. This energetic advocate of
leisure had kept the *Atlantic* supplied with a steady succession of
short works and had often contributed to other periodicals. In 1942
the best of these selections, along with some written in the late
1920s, were published in a volume entitled *Under a Thatched Roof*,
the first such collection by Hall since *Mid-Pacific* in 1928.

The book begins with "A Word for the Essayist," a paean to
those old-fashioned authors who have kept the essay alive in an age
of less traditional and more utilitarian forms such as the editorial
and the article. It is not surprising that Hall, who since the First
World War had been expressing his discomfort with the ever-
accelerating pace of life that industry and technology were foisting
upon mankind, should have praised the essay for being a bulwark
against the ravages of modernity. It is a bit startling, however, to
find this native of Colfax, resident of Tahiti, and lifelong hater of
cities asserting that essayists are indispensable to society because in
times of crisis "they somehow hold fast to urbanity."[1] It is even
more jarring when this extoller of primitive life in the South Seas
proceeds to exclaim: "When urbanity decays, civilization suffers
and decays with it" (6).

Yet, for all his adoration of Polynesia, Hall had never been an unequivocal primitivist. If he loved simple islanders, he also doted on
authors who were anything but simple—Cervantes, Chaucer,
Lamb, Conrad. His tastes in music inclined more toward the
nineteenth-century symphony than toward savage chants. And the
Anglophilia which had blazed from the pages of his first book,
flickered throughout his subsequent works, and which glows forth
in some of the later selections in *Under a Thatched Roof* hardly

betokens a man for whom "civilization" was a pejorative word. It was not an antipathy toward civilization that had driven Hall from the Western world to the South Pacific. It was, rather, his aversion to a new barbarism which he believed rampant industrialism and commerce were engendering in Europe and America. Furthermore, for Hall, as for Thomas Jefferson, urbanity was by no means contingent upon urbanization. Indeed, for him the two were almost antithetical. In fact the point of this essay is that a truly urbane author must be at odds with the tenor of modern life, which is overwhelmingly city life. Hall believes that such an author will find that eighteenth-century relic, the essay, more congenial than its twentieth-century offspring, the article and editorial. Is it astonishing, then, that Hall should have preferred a South Sea island to New York and Los Angeles?

The next selection, "Talk," records a conversation between Hall and Nordhoff in Tahiti. Although they begin by discussing Robert Frost, they soon pass on to other matters which reveal the essential differences between the two men. Nordhoff, for example, praises hard work. Hall defends idleness. Nordhoff retorts that such lotus-eating nonsense is the result of Hall's "rambling in the hills so often" (13). In response to Nordhoff's inquiry as to what he thinks about up there, Hall replies that he has acquired "the habit of reverie." Nordhoff maintains that such reverie might be dangerous and explains that, unlike his friend, he has come to the South Seas not for solitude but because he likes fishing in tropical waters and "going to seed slowly and pleasantly" (16). He goes on to insist that both of them have deteriorated in Tahiti, but that the place is now the only home he has. Hall, always the Iowan, says he is still a Midwesterner at heart and will never cease to be one however much he might love Polynesia. Although the colloquy ends on an amiable note, there is a disturbing echo of Kurtz's dying words, "The horror! The horror!" in Joseph Conrad's *The Heart of Darkness* when Nordhoff exclaims: "Oh, the decay, the decay in houses and men in this humid tropical climate!" (21).

It may seem incongruous that Hall, the more prolific of the two writers, should have been extolling idleness while Nordhoff was advocating hard work. But back in 1928 when the conversation occurred, Nordhoff's career had been faring better than his friend's. Perhaps Hall delayed publishing "Talk" until 1942 because he was waiting for the years to validate his contention that reverie was beneficial and that living in the tropics need not cause a deterioration of one's faculties. If so, by that date Hall had certainly found his vindication in the twenty books he had already produced, half of them without Nordhoff's assistance.

Hall, though, was individualistic enough not to expect everyone to emulate him. The next selection, "Knight's House," is an account of his futile efforts to impose one of his own values on a friend. This man, Knight, has a house in a remote part of the island—a thing of beauty outside but inside a marvel of filth and chaos. One day, while Knight is away, Hall slips in and tidies up the place only to become uneasy because he feels that he has obliterated his friend's personality. Thus, when the house reverts to its formerly squalid condition, Hall is almost pleased.

"To the Ice Mountain" is not, as one might suppose, a reprinting of one of Hall's Iceland travel sketches but an elaborate dream fantasy. Most of the action transpires in China, suggested to him by a picture he has obtained from a restaurant proprietor in Papeete. Into the Arcadian oriental scene comes Lafcadio Hearn, one of Hall's favorite authors. Soon Hall's son, Conrad, whose middle name is Lafcadio, appears, as do three venerable Chinese sages who, after uttering words of wisdom, provide Hall with paper and ink. He is, however, unable to write but finally manages to eke out something, complaining in the process how difficult it is to please readers of travel literature. China then turns into the reading room of the Reykjavik Library, where he sits thinking of Amy Lowell's "Lilacs" just before his son awakens him.

The major point of this piece, of course, is that the mind is not confined by the boundaries of time and space. The work also provides a glimpse into the tensions between Hall's creative impulses, his inhibitions as an author, and the wishes of his public. "To the Ice Mountain" also extolls the essay as a form at the expense of fiction. At one point one of the Chinese sages says that the novel has practically crushed the essay. But the essay, he asserts, will ultimately triumph because "it is really far more durable and valuable than fiction, in the majority of cases" (39). Hall states that he shares the sage's preferences but not his certainty that the essay will prevail.

In "The Scribbling Mania" Hall examines the compulsion writers as a group have for putting words on paper. He rejects Arthur Machen's contention that the source of this urge is a longing to escape from the horrors of life. Life, Hall insists, is not all that terrible. Furthermore, writing itself can be an agonizing experience. He then touches upon a point he had treated extensively in an article entitled "Too Many Books"—that too many people in the modern world feel compelled to write. Thus, Hall is alarmed to find proliferation, the beast that technology has loosed upon the globe, afflicting even his own profession. Yet, for all his misgivings, he is resigned to enduring the consequent deluge of drivel on the grounds that unpromising writers sometimes later do valuable work. Hall's resignation was sustained, no doubt, by his recollection of the many rejections his own writings had elicited before he was to achieve even a minimal success.

Of "Happy Endings" we shall say little beyond noting that in it Hall parodies several types of pessimistic short stories in vogue during the Great Depression. The parodies abound in Thurberesque twists and absurd juxtapositions and conclude with preposterous happy solutions to what are often serious problems. The stories are all quite amusing, but their humor defies summary or excerpting.

On the other hand, "A Small Dissenting Voice" is full of passages which could be quoted profitably. Since most of them, however, state aspects of the same major point—that modern life is changing too rapidly—we can limit ourselves to a few of Hall's most cogent comments. After proclaiming his own attachment to bygone days, he says he fears that "there are no past-minded men any more in America" (78). He is especially disturbed by the manner in which links that unite generations have been broken in the United States.

He is also troubled by the despoilation of nature, and it does not take him long, of course, to direct special scorn at that offspring of industry he loathed above all others, "that worst of abominations, the automobile," which he blamed for having destroyed the identity as well as the "charm and peace" of "remote villages and rural communities" (80). At the conclusion of the essay, however, he once again makes it clear that his major objection to industrialism is not its materialism per se but the giddy pace of life it engenders. When change becomes too rapid, he suggests, both society and individuals suffer. And, in his final words, he asserts that in the United States the rate of change has passed the danger point.

Comment on this essay seems almost superfluous. Its central theme is so integral to Hall's philosophy that it is at least a peripheral element in just about everything he wrote. The only uncharacteristic feature is the unremitting severity of its tone. A parenthetical note at the conclusion goes far toward accounting for that severity—(New York City, 1928). By that year Hall's fortunes had not yet taken much of an upward turn. As for New York, Hall, who disliked cities in general, had a particularly intense antipathy toward that behemoth among American metropolises.

In fact, in the next essay, "The Spirit of Place," he signals out New York for special contumely. In Chicago on the elevated railway Hall has known "the silence of a vastness of a presence that says 'I am!' " He has experienced a similar presence in Kansas City and Denver. But the vast city on the Hudson River—a city where "one is conscious of no mighty influence superior to the works of man"—is a paradigm of the sterility and lack of cohesion of the modern industrial world (88).

Almost antithetical to New York in this respect is Iceland, the subject of the next offering. "*Skip*: A Strong Icelandic Noun" is an amusing account of Hall's inability to master the intricacies of Icelandic grammar during his sojourn in that northern land. The humor here is directed overtly at the author himself. Yet beneath it lurks a joke at the expense of Sir Francis Bacon, rationalist *par excellence* and avatar of modern science. Hall quotes from Bacon's essay "Of Travel"—"He that travelleth into a country before he hath not some entrance into the language, goeth to school and not to travel." Shamed by Bacon's admonition, Hall sets about to learn Icelandic but makes a botch of it. The reader, however, is left with the impression that Hall's time would have been spent more valuably roaming about the countryside storing up impressions of a sort for which there was no place in the English philosopher's scheme of things.

There would have been ample room for such impressions, though, in the philosophy of the subject of the next essay, Henry David Thoreau. In "A Belated Rebuttal" Hall attempts to refute Robert Louis Stevenson's disparagements of Thoreau, a favorite of Hall's (as, for that matter, Stevenson was). The major point of contention is Stevenson's disapproval of Thoreau's solitary ways. Hall, of course, firmly believed solitude to be beneficial unless pursued with fanaticism. Hall's admiration of Thoreau is not difficult to understand. Although an amiable man with many friends, Hall shared Thoreau's love of contemplation and privacy as well as his sometimes quirky individualism. To be sure he had little of Thoreau's disdain for tradition. But Hall, excoriator of automobiles and radios, must have felt himself a spiritual descendent of the man who in *Walden* had written that our "inventions are wont to be pretty toys" and whose response to the impending construction of a telegraph from Maine to Texas was to suggest that those two states may have had "nothing important to communicate."

"Three Chance Meetings" is a diverting anecdote about how Hall, under the most improbable circumstances, encounters fellow former airmen in Papeete and New York. Apart from its value as entertainment, it is interesting in that it contains something perhaps unique in Hall's huge output: an almost complimentary statement about New York. He says that whenever he is in that city he invariably spends a day in one of the railroad terminals delighting in the crowds, the color, and the excitement. Probably, though, these words are less a compliment to the city than to the mode of transportation he had loved so much as a boy in Iowa. There is nothing equivocal, however, about his comments in this selection upon another subject—the merits of his own first book, *Kitchener's Mob*. Although he does not refer to the title, he establishes its identity by indication that he had given a copy to a friend in 1916, two years before the publication of his second book, *High Adventure*. He does report, however, that his friend rejected Hall's harsh assessment of the work. So does the author of this study.

In "A Neglected Art" Hall again praises idling and upbraids Henry Ford, who epitomized all that Hall disliked about the modern world. After castigating Ford for having said that there is no place in civilization for the idler, Hall points out that the country is suffering from the disastrous effects of industry's rampant growth while "leisure is becoming a wasted raw material" (137). The bane of the United States, he asserts, is that it contains so few "professors" of the art of leisure. In fact, the only ones of the first rank he can identify are Frost, Thoreau, and Whitman. He sees the source of the contagion not as some unique flaw in the American character but as the Western notion that all scientific ideas must be put to practical use. Indeed, he regards the father of most of our present ills as none other than Sir Francis Bacon.

The main idea here Hall had been expressing as far back as *Faery Lands of the South Seas*. But perhaps nowhere else does he focus his displeasure so sharply upon Western civilization's compulsion to act under the aegis of scientific progress regardless of how destructive the actions may be. For him, rationalists like Ford and Bacon are the true madmen: driven creatures who, in their pursuit of knowledge and technological innovation, trample upon everything in nature and society which makes life agreeable. To make matters worse, these men insist upon inducting all of humanity into their

legions of seekers and doers. Thus they have turned most of Europe
and America into vast armies of frenzied automatons. It is no
wonder, therefore, that he was convinced that contemplative persons such as himself had to seek refuge in whatever byways they
could find: only there could they preserve their identities and keep
alive values essential to the spiritual well-being of mankind.

The next offering, "On the Far Side of the Island," consists of
several vignettes which suggest that life on Tahiti is everything that
life in Europe and America is not—leisurely, tranquil, and healthy.
In one sketch he discovers a watch he had lost back in 1920 and
realizes how fortunate he has been to have learned to live without
it. In another he spies a hermit crab retreating into its shell and
notes that the earth would be a better place if industrialists had
emulated it by giving more time to loafing and reflecting. Once,
when Hall joins a native in gathering wild bananas in the mountains, he is put to shame by his primitive companion's robust frame
and strong feet. In the concluding sketch Hall, watching Polynesian
children splashing in the water, is saddened by the thought of the
future effects of Western technology upon his beloved island. But,
never one to succumb to a sense of futility, he comforts himself by
supposing that "a thousand years hence cocks will crow, as of old,
awakening children to bathe in the sea" (153).

It is certainly more than fortuitous that the foregoing paean to
Polynesian tranquility should be followed by an essay entitled "The
State of Being Bored." Hall, anything but a fool, certainly realized
that the principal objection most people would have to the simple
contemplative life he extolled is that it would quickly pall. His solu-
tion to the problem of boredom is simple and characteristic—sub-
mission. Unlike acedia—an utter despair curable only by
death—boredom is, he contends, a transitory malady. It will resist,
however, all deliberate attempts to dispel it. The best we can do is
to prepare for our attacks with fortitude and to endure them. This
essay, no less than those denouncing rampant industrialization,
challenges Western man's belief that the proper response to every
problem is to resort to some kind of purposeful activity. The fortitude that Hall recommends has none of the blustering asser-
tiveness we associate with Theodore Roosevelt. It is more akin to
the heroic acquiescence of the Stoics.

Two criticisms could be made. Not everybody has Hall's capacity
for enduring unpleasant states of consciousness. Furthermore, not
many people have Hall's compensation, a profession that enabled

him to exorcise those states by expressing them. Whether we accept
his overall argument, however, probably will depend upon whether
we assent to his premise that boredom, no less than the Kingdom of
God, is within us. If we do, we shall agree that there are no boring
places, only bored individuals who will suffer wherever they reside
or whatever they do. Hall's conclusion, therefore, will seem a
truism—wise men will endure boredom because they must endure
it. As for those who reject the premise, they are likely to find Hall's
entire world-view so unpalatable that they would not get far enough
into *Under a Thatched Roof* to read this essay.

The next selection makes a perfect companion piece to its
predecessor. In "Happiness" Hall contends that bliss, no less than
boredom, can well up within us spontaneously. There seems to be
this difference: whereas boredom can strike any place under just
about any circumstances, Hall reports that he has never experienced
one of his gratuitous spells of blessedness in a city. Furthermore,
these visitations, as Hall calls them, usually descended upon him
during periods of idleness and amid natural surroundings back in
rural Iowa or in Tahiti. In these two works Hall says, in effect: let us
not fight our psyches. Let us drift along with them because they
have their own rhythms and offer rewards which more than com-
pensate for whatever vexations they bring us. We should resign
ourselves to their grimmer moods because such moods will pass of
their own accord. But if we remain receptive they will reward us
with exaltations of a kind we could never will into being. Yet we
must aid our psyches a bit. Being a part of nature, they are apt to
malfunction in those places which mankind has erected in its misguided war upon nature.

One final point must be made about "Happiness." Although in it
Hall describes a mental state that savors of mysticism, he insists that
his visitations are "definitely concerned with this good earth" and
then maintains that he would experience them more often if possible because he could "wish for no heaven save this one that we
have" (161). This is not an appropriate place for a lengthy discussion of Hall's religious opinions. Yet a far more cursory summary of
this essay than the one we have presented here should make it apparent that Hall's temperament was reverential. He envisioned
nature and the soul of man as governed by forces essentially benign.
It should be equally apparent that his veneration of those forces
owed far more to the pantheism of Wordsworth and the
Transcendentalism of Thoreau, two of his favorite authors, than it

owed to the Protestant theology he had been exposed to in his youth. For Hall nature was not tainted by original sin, only by Western man's defilement of it in pursuit of "progress." He believed that for the person receptive to the promptings of his own soul and to the bounty of nature, paradise was not lost—only camouflaged.

The next work can be passed over quickly. We should note, however, that "The Hat" in its jocular way reinforces the theme of the two more serious essays we have just examined: that we should be true to our own nature as well as to nature. Thus when, in this anecdote, he permits a salesman to cow him into purchasing an expensive hat inharmonious with his character, Hall feels he deserves the mirth he evokes in bystanders when the incongruous item goes flying off on the breeze.

In "Tunnelled Pages" Hall uses an account of how worms are devouring books in his library in Tahiti as a pretext for commenting on some of his favorite authors. The first of these is Ben Jonson, whom he believes to be insufficiently appreciated. To Hall it is irrelevant that much of Jonson's "wisdom is derived from Greek and Latin authors" because true wisdom for Hall must echo the past, since humanity remains essentially the same throughout the ages. A mention of Coleridge's "Rime of the Ancient Mariner" affords Hall an opportunity to thrust at the scholarly mind when he observes that, although John Livingston Lowes's *The Road to Xanadu* accounts for the origins of Coleridge's imagery, the mystery of creation remains unresolved. Joseph Conrad not surprisingly receives the most attention. Particularly noteworthy is the praise Hall bestows upon the Pole's use of tales within tales and upon his mastery of the art of digression—devices Hall hardly eschewed in his own writings. Hall is contemptuous of H. G. Wells's dismissal of Conrad (and of Stephen Crane and Henry James) for lacking a scientific education. Hall asserts that if Wells's "planned world" ever comes into being mankind will need "a few unredeemed of the James and Conrad kind" (185). The essay, though, ends in a major key with Hall's proclaiming that in fiction he likes earthy characters such as Huck Finn, Joseph in *Wuthering Heights*, Sam Weller, and John Fry and that "life is as good now as it was in their days" and will remain so if leaders cease doing their utmost to make the world intolerable (186). Of course "Tunnelled Pages," with its subjectivity and impressionism, is as remote from most academic criticism as it could be—for which Hall, a man of common sense thoroughly devoid of pedantry, would have been grateful.

"Trains" is a hymn to Hall's favorite method of transportation. And because hymns must be sung and cannot be paraphrased, we cannot hope to convey its character without quoting it in its entirety, an obvious impossibility. We must explain, though, why Hall should have exempted the railroad alone among the products of technology from his disapproval. His explanation is that, unlike other machines, the steam locomotive seems human. It breathes and has moods like a man or woman. A deeper reason, however, seems to be that the railroad was inextricably entwined with Hall's memories of his boyhood in Iowa.

The essay also contains one of Hall's most explicit statements about the ambivalence of his attitude toward Colfax (here called Prairie Hills). After confessing to a yearning to leave the place as a child, he says: "Now that I look back on it from sufficient distance, I would not have had that boyhood, nor the town where it was spent, changed in any particular" (194). There is, of course, a poignancy to the paradox here of a man looking back longingly at his boyhood self who had longed to do what the man had done—leave home. To be sure, Hall in a sense never left rural Iowa because he bore it in his memory throughout his life and regained many of its most cherished qualities in the South Seas. Yet neither memory nor replacement could efface his sense of loss, as the following passage about the cry of a train whistle on the prairie reveals: "I can hear it, even on this island in the mid-Pacific, and a kind of melancholy seizes me as though it were the last train we are ever to see or hear, on its last journey—into the past" (199).

The penultimate essay in the volume, "Mr. Smith's Umbrella," expresses Hall's support for England in its struggle against Nazi Germany. England, under whose banner Hall had fought for more than a year in the earlier worldwide conflict, epitomized for him those humane and urbane values he most admired in its writers. And the umbrella which the English man of letters, Logan Pearsall Smith, clung to during London's travail became for Hall a symbol of Britain's staid indomitability. This work contains what may be Hall's fiercest denunciation of Germany. In his writings about World War I, even those he wrote while his comrades were dying, he was often astonishingly charitable toward the Germans. Now, however, incensed by their conduct under Hitler's leadership, he

resorted to language uncharacteristically vehement. Germany and
its ally Japan, he insisted, guided by "the diabolical doctrine" that
man must "the hammer or anvil be," must themselves "be made
anvils and beaten" until they learned to "accept the doctrine, Live
and let Live" (206).

It may seem anticlimactic to have ended such a book with a light
essay that, in addition to recounting Hall's inability to emulate
Anthony Trollope's work schedule, disparages James Joyce's
Ulysses. Yet, if England embodied many of the political and
cultural values Hall admired, Joyce represented the literary values
he most disliked. And it was in his aesthetic preferences that Hall
diverged most acutely from his major contemporary authors. After
all, few writers of consequence have been enamored of the political
and economic contours of the twentieth century. And Hall was
hardly unique in preferring a bygone era to the present or in favor-
ing some less-developed area of the globe over industrialized
Europe and America. But however much authors like Pound, Eliot,
Yeats, Lawrence, and Jeffers may have loathed the modern world,
they were avid in pursuit of modernity in their own art. This oft-
noted blend of literary radicalism with conservative or reactionary
politics has been one of the more bizarre incongruities of early and
mid-twentieth-century intellectual life. It is a blend that Hall eschewed. The obscure, the perverse, the strident repelled him on
paper as they repelled him in a person or a society. Moreover, he
perceived rampant experimentalism in literature, like technological
proliferation, as an assault on stability, simplicity, and continuity—qualities he regarded as essential to the health of individuals and nations. Thus, if Hall was correct, twentieth-century
aesthetics have been as misguided as twentieth-century politics.

Under a Thatched Roof demonstrates that a decade of writing fiction had not diminished Hall's mastery of the essay and the sketch.
In their adroit balance between discursiveness and incisiveness,
humor and seriousness, the selections in this volume are at least
equal to those in *Mid-Pacific* and *On the Stream of Travel*. The fact
that *Under a Thatched Roof* was the only one of these collections to
be in print in 1978 certainly does not prove its superiority to the
others. Yet the volume does surpass its predecessors in two respects:
(1) it presents a view of the world that in general seems wiser and
more mature; (2) it has a broader scope.

In *Mid-Pacific* and *On the Stream of Travel* Hall's rejection of
the modern industrial world sometimes seems more the result of

youthful recklessness than of a reasoned rejection of comprehended evils. In those earlier works he often dons the persona of a young innocent—part Candide, part Huck Finn—who submits to every whim. Off he will go anywhere, any time, if adventure beckons. In fact his readiest antidote for travail is travel. Thus without a second's hesitation he will head for Iceland, run home to Iowa, return to Tahiti, set off for the Tuamotus. If he runs out of money or if his garden abounds in weeds rather than in vegetables, he worries not. Like Micawber he is convinced that something will turn up, as something invariably does.

The persona is an engaging one, and it does embody facets of Hall's character, albeit it caricatures them; but it impedes the serious strain in him, and it hardly enhances his credibility when he addresses himself to major problems. In *Under a Thatched Roof*, however, his persona has been modified. The charm is still there. So are the tolerance and the good humor. But the voice that speaks to us is not that of an impulsive innocent but of a self-styled "old-fogey"—more wary, more pensive. The change, of course, reflects actuality. Hall in the 1930s and 1940s was no longer an insouciant adventurer and struggling writer. Now he was a famous, happily married, highly productive author. Not all writers are improved by success, and many men learn little from experience. Hall, though, had thrived on recognition, as his friend Nordhoff had not. Then, too, new responsibilities and fresh impressions had widened the spectrum of colors on his palette—hence, the multihued richness of *Under a Thatched Roof*.

II   *Vive la France!*

Men Without Country was Hall's most tangible contribution to the Allied effort in World War II as well as his sole contribution to the movie career of Humphrey Bogart. Of the film version, titled *Passage to Marseilles*, we need say nothing. As for the book, which was mostly Hall's work even though Nordhoff's name also appeared on the cover, it is not bad as such efforts go. The basic premise of the plot, to be sure, is somewhat implausible: a group of convicts escape from the penal colony in Cayenne and endure all manner of ordeals at sea to offer their services to the Free French forces in England. But if we accept the premise, most of what follows is effective enough as an adventure tale. The book even contains some felicities of a sort rarely found in wartime propaganda.

Among the more interesting features of *Men Without Country* is
that it reveals an even greater sympathy for criminals than Hall and
his partner had exhibited in *Botany Bay*. Employing the story-
within-a-story device to which Hall was partial, the novel glorifies
the exploits of a band of escaped prisoners and denigrates Major
Duval, an odious martinet, who represents the forces the Allies are
fighting against.

After the convicts are rescued from their canoe by the France-
bound cargo vessel, *Ville de Nancy*, Duval demands that the captain lock them up and turn them over to the police in Marseilles.
Captain Malo refuses on the grounds that they might really be, as
they contend, gold miners from Venezuela. Malo, in turn, is supported by the narrator, Captain Freycinet, a former wine merchant
who, despite his age and his excess weight, has been serving as a
nonflying c.o. in the French Air Force. Freycinet soon begins to
suspect that Duval is correct about the castaways. But so antipathetic is he toward Duval that he not only continues to side with
the men but actually warns them of Duval's suspicions, whereupon
they confess that they are indeed escaped convicts and proceed to
tell him their story.

Suffice it to say that, although their backgrounds and degrees of
criminal culpability vary considerably, all five are brave, strong,
sympathetic figures. The most important are Maillot and Matrac.
The former, a deserter in World War I, compensates for his earlier
cowardice by becoming the boldest Communist agitator in Paris,
willing to take any risk for his cause. Eventually he is arrested and
sentenced to Cayenne for fifteen years through the machinations of
the right-wing *Croix de Feu*. The other, Matrac, is described as the
"most remarkable of the band"—a man of "unbreakable spirit
whom no guard could cow and who forced even the prison
authorities to respect him."[2]

The upshot of all this is a confrontation between Duval and his
supporters, on the one hand, and Freycinet, Malo, and the convicts
on the other, over whether to take the ship to England and join the
Free French there or to sail to Marseilles, then under the banner of
Pétain's Vichy regime. The noble outlaws and their cohorts prevail.
Maillot later becomes wireless operator on the *Ville de Nancy*,
which, en route to Canada, is torpedoed. Matrac becomes an ace
tail gunner who dies of wounds received during a raid on Berlin. As
for Freycinet, he lives on to narrate the story to a *New York Times*
correspondent named Manning.

Some explanation should be made for Hall's sympathetic por-

trayal of the Communist, Maillot. It would be erroneous to assume
that Hall, always impervious to fashions, was succumbing to the
Marxist fad rampant among intellectuals during the 1930s and early
1940s. As a man who detested sudden and massive change, he was
hardly likely to be attracted even fleetingly to a movement com-
mitted to worldwide revolution. Moreover, as one who looked
askance at panaceas and who hated authoritarianism, he would
never have been enamored of a utopian ideology whose proponents
were given to totalitarian practices. There is no reason to believe,
furthermore, that the anti-Stalinist sentiments he expressed a few
years afterwards in *A Word for His Sponsor* resulted from a reversal
of his earlier opinions on the matter. Two factors, however, should
be borne in mind. The first is that during the war Communist
Russia, then the sole bastion of communism, was allied with Britain,
the United States, and the Free French—a fact anti-Red witch-
hunters of the late 1940s and 1950s seemed eager to ignore. The
second point is that *Men Without Country* is constructed around a
moral and political paradox: that in a corrupt and betrayed country
such as France was in the late 1930s and early 1940s categories such
as treason and loyalty, justice and injustice, lost their normal
definitions. Bad men mouth good principles, and good men serve
bad causes.

The notion Hall propounds in *Men Without Country*, that when
times are askew the enemies of a society are apt to represent its
finest qualities, may be a debatable one. But it provides a more
provocative theme than we generally encounter in war books or in
the movies derived from them. Although the framework Hall
employs sometimes seems simplistic, the moral ambiguities he
offers keep the book from being simpleminded—no mean achievement in a work of its genre.

III *Paradise Defiled*

If Nordhoff made a minimal contribution to *Men Without Country*, he made none whatever to *Lost Island*. First published in 1944,
the latter work was Hall's first lone venture as a novelist (unless we
categorize his volume of eighteenth-century tall tales, *Doctor
Dogbody's Leg*, as a novel). Gone are the plot contrivances, the
sudden reversals, the last-moment rescues of the books he wrote
with Nordhoff. As in his sketches, Hall in *Lost Island* unfolds his
story in a leisurely, discursive manner.

Although the plot is amorphous it derives considerable thrust from its central incident, the impending destruction of a Polynesian island in order to convert it into an American air base during World War II. We may know what is going to occur, but we do not know in advance what the circumstances and consequences of the destruction will be. As the novel develops, it makes a point worth our attention: that Western civilization, in pursuit of admirable objectives, often disrupts the lives of inoffensive people and destroys cultures and places of natural beauty. Hall's book, as a result, is, in the words of Richard Match, a "miniature tragedy of all the world's bewildered, uprooted lives." Diana Trilling also found *Lost Island* tragic and commented approvingly on its exposure of the cruel paradox by which Western nations have contrived "a strange world . . . in which we have to destroy civilization in order to preserve it."[3]

Thus Hall demonstrates in this novel that, despite his oft-stated optimism, he was able to confront a tragic dilemma unflinchingly. In *Lost Island* he offers no facile solutions, no moral oversimplifications. One of Hall's Polynesian Edens is to be defaced by military barracks and overrun by American soldiers and sailors. Perhaps Richard Match is correct in contending that Hall's explanation of the tragedy—that "industrial civilization is to blame for the horrors and unavoidable destructiveness of modern warfare"—is somewhat naive.[4] But if Hall errs in making industrialism the cause of all that is destructive in modern life, it can hardly be denied that industrialism has been the principal instrument of destruction. With the most malevolent intentions, a medieval prince could not have wrought, in so brief a time, a fraction of the carnage and cultural dislocation inflicted during World War II by even the most benevolent of participating industrial powers. Moreover, the machine is certainly a valid symbol for all that is inhuman in the modern world. Hall's bulldozers, therefore, are symbolic brothers of the tractors in *The Grapes of Wrath*, the planes and tanks in *For Whom the Bell Tolls*, and the nightmarish conveyor belt in Chaplin's *Modern Times*.

During the war, Hall saw his beloved islands menaced by invading fleets and gutted by concrete airstrips. The invaders, however, were not the hated Axis nations but his compatriots, the Americans, for the Japanese naval power never extended to the Society Islands where Hall resided and, indeed, left the Polynesian groups, in general, untouched. The United States, however, needing air and naval bases to pursue its war with Japan in the

Western Pacific, naturally turned to the islands farther west administered to by allies, principally Britain or de Gaullist France. Now, however dissatisfied with Western civilization Hall may have been, he never ceased to be loyal to his native country. Moreover, his sympathies during World War II were unequivocally with the Allied cause.

The hero of *Lost Island*, therefore, as an engineer with the inescapable duty of disrupting the tranquility of an island he loves, perfectly embodies Hall's own dilemma. George Dodd, devoted to his country, believes in its cause yet wishes that inoffensive Edens could remain untouched by the outside world. He realizes, however, that when powerless communities stand in the path of mighty conflicts, those communities will be trampled upon. As a compassionate observer, he may weep, but he cannot effectively intervene. And indeed he believes he should not intervene because he is convinced that the interests of mankind in general require that these innocents be sacrificed.

To make matters worse, Dodd believes that the holocaust, ready at last to strike even the most remote lands, is as much the result of American, British, and French timidity and unpreparedness as of German and Japanese military aggressiveness: "I thought with a bitterness common to all of us in these days of the so-called statesmen who, until it was too late, remained so blindly indifferent to all the repeated warnings and danger signals."[5]

Yet, while conceding the need to confront political and military dangers and while recognizing that technological growth will continue, Hall does not renounce his allegiance to the values represented by Polynesia. He admits that most Americans do not share those values. But, speaking through George Dodd, he insists that, once the Axis Powers have been defeated, the people who love solitude, leisure, and simplicity should strive for the "freedom to enjoy life on a human scale, on a planet not wholly wrecked and desolated by machines." He then proceeds to deplore what "the world may be coming to if we go on as we are going now" and to hope wistfully that, after the war, parts of the earth will "be walled off, so to speak: out of bounds to explorers and all their allied tribes" (6 - 7)—a hope that he does not entertain, he confesses, very optimistically.

Lost Island, therefore, records the climax of the tragedy that is incipient in Herman Melville's *Typee* and *Omoo*. By the 1940s Polynesian culture had been moribund for nearly a century. Yet, on

a remote atoll here, in an isolated valley there, enough remained of
the old ways for Hall to glean the glories of the past. Moreover,
despite the demise of native traditions, one essential factor
remained—peace. Whatever else civilization had done to the South
Pacific, it had not shattered the tranquility of the islands. War,
mechanization, efficiency experts, and other curses of life in Europe
and America were thousands of miles away. Suddenly, with an impact greater than that of the storm which Hall and Nordhoff had
described in *The Hurricane*, all that was most terrible in Western
civilization descended upon island after island in Polynesia. The
hills and groves of Eden were leveled by bulldozers; Polynesian
Eves became lovers of American airmen and marines. The great
world, in short, invaded Hall's little world and gave him an opportunity to make his old theme universal.

In *Lost Island*, he used that opportunity to what was probably the
best of his ability. No *deus ex machina* saves the island as it saves
Terangi in *The Hurricane*; no fantasy mutes the horror of reality for
Dodd as it was to do for Alec Brooke in *The High Barbaree*. The
island becomes not a refuge but simply one more ravaged community in a world where no place is safe. Not the least of the merits
of *Lost Island* is that it does not sentimentalize the plight of the
natives. In fact, after Dodd in the epilogue describes the more unpleasant consequences of the American occupation of the island,
one of his auditors laughs. Dodd smiles and observes: "There is,
often, something intrinsically comic in tragic situations" (207). It is
possible that Hall sensed that, in the machine-afflicted twentieth
century, even tragedy somehow becomes, in its vast impersonality,
something less than tragic. Whether he sensed this possibility or
not, one thing is certain: *Lost Island* does not evade the principal
issues it raises. Hall, like Dodd, may not completely abandon his
dream of a Polynesian paradise, but he does not allow the dream to
impair his perception of the ugliest realities of modern life and
death.

IV   *End of the Partnership*

The High Barbaree, the final work to bear the names of both
Nordhoff and Hall, reveals few traces of the former's work. To be
sure, Hall had done the greater portion of the writing in their
preceding novel. But, whether because Nordhoff's suggestions had
often prevailed or because Hall successfully initiated their earlier

collaborative efforts, *Men Without Country* exhibits some of Nordhoff's characteristics; *The High Barbaree* seems all Hall.

Unfortunately in it Hall uses a narrative design which stifles his most appealing qualities—his humor, his ripened wisdom, his common sense—and which magnifies other traits so much that they become parodies of themselves. Thus his discursiveness turns into loquacity, and his nostalgia for Iowa and his South Seas primitivism seem escapism.

Once again he uses the story-within-a-story device. As the book begins two young American pilots are clinging to the floating body of their aircraft, which has been shot down over the Pacific by a Japanese submarine. One of the pilots, Gene Mauriac, a Californian like Nordhoff, serves a single function—to listen to the life story of his companion, Alec Brooke. Like Hall, Brooke is a native of Iowa and a graduate of Grinnell College. What this means, in effect, is that the first half or so of the novel is a romanticized autobiography of Hall. One of the principal incidents, in fact, actually was to appear in Hall's memoir, *My Island Home*. When, halfway through the book, Mauriac dies, Hall converts Alec Brooke's reminiscences into a soliloquy. Then, lo! What should loom on the horizon but the island he has heard about as a child from his Uncle Thad: Turnbull's Island or, as Alec prefers to call it, The High Barbaree. Here it is—an island absent from most maps, a realm of peace and beauty. Washed ashore, Alec discovers there a kindly missionary and gentle, wise Polynesians. Next to appear are Uncle Thad and Alec's childhood sweetheart, Nancy (the name, incidentally, of Hall's daughter). Alec and Nancy marry. Then the point of view shifts. A patrol plane sights the floating wreckage of Alec and Gene's aircraft; the bodies of both young men are found. Alec's sojourn on the High Barbaree has been merely the dream of a dying lover of tranquility killed by a war-mad world.

There are three basic problems with all this: Alec is too young and callow to be Hall's surrogate; Alec's pre-World War II Iowa is not interchangeable with Hall's turn-of-the-century one; and the island is too idyllic to be even interesting let alone plausible.

What usually makes Hall's literary ruminations effective is that they are patently the work of a cultivated, extensively traveled, widely read man able to contrast present events with numerous and varied past ones. We are delighted to have him talk about himself because he has such a rich fund of recollections to draw upon—and also because his diffident sense of humor keeps his reminiscing from seeming egotistical. Brooke, lacking these advantages, should not be narrating a story in Hall's manner.

As for the Iowa episodes, they lose much of their cogency by being set shortly before World War II. A point which Hall makes repeatedly in his works is that after 1918 rural America, because of the advent of technological monstrosities such as the automobile, had ceased being idyllic. Thus whereas Hall's late nineteenth- and early-twentieth century prairie village could represent values at variance with those modern forces which were destroying peace, simplicity, and order everywhere, Brooke's boyhood community cannot do so.

The difficulty with Alec's dream island is just the opposite: it embodies Hall's and Alec's values too perfectly. Even an ideal realm must have some plausibility if we are to accept it as a tenable alternative to reality. Although in his travel sketches Hall sometimes would idealize the Tuamotus or Tahiti, he would people them with credible human beings, white and brown, with foibles as well as charms. Thus in the sketches he imparts to his ideal enough imperfections and tangibility to render it interesting and credible—something he does not do with Alec's island.

The High Barbaree has other blemishes. Hall's friend, Robert Dean Frisbie, noted two of them in a letter to Hall:

Who chlorinated the last part of this wish-fulfillment dream: Was it you or Nordhoff? The ceremony should have ended with the old Polynesian service. . . . Why bring the parson in? I also object to the ending. You seem to have been afraid that your readers would not realize that the entire island part of your story is Alec's dream while dying.[6]

Yet, despite its imperfections, anyone sympathetic to Hall's vision of life is likely to find *The High Barbaree* touching. To risk validating at least the first half of Vladimir Nabokov's contention that whenever a critic refers to a writer's sincerity either the critic or the writer is a fool, we must observe that Hall's earnestness is appealing. No reader of *The High Barbaree* is apt to question the intensity of Hall's aversion to modern warfare, his love of tranquility and the South Pacific, his affection for the Iowa of his boyhood, and his horror over what was happening in the 1940s to the world and to people who only wanted to be left in peace. Fortunately he expressed these admirable sentiments more effectively in other works.

CHAPTER 10

Coda

TWO years after the publication of *The High Barbaree*, Nordhoff died. Although the end came suddenly, caused by a heart attack, he had suffered intermittently from poor health for nearly a decade. His final years, spent mainly in his native California, had been marred by a series of business misadventures. Neither had he fared well with his writing. As we have seen, the last books to bear his name had been mostly Hall's work; furthermore, Nordhoff's attempts to collaborate with another author had been abortive.

Hall was to outlive him by only slightly more than four years. Even though at the time of his partner's death he seemed to be flourishing in every way, his own health soon began to deteriorate. During a visit to the United States in 1950 to attend a class reunion at Grinnell College, which was to confer upon him an honorary doctorate, he suffered from numbness in his left leg. A medical examination in Boston revealed that he had arteriosclerosis. The following year, back in Tahiti, he died, as Nordhoff had done, of heart failure.

Hall's last years, however, were by no means unhappy or unproductive. During them he saw his daughter, Nancy, married; and his son, Conrad, was graduated from the University of Southern California the same month as Hall was granted an honorary doctorate by Grinnell College. He lived to complete his most ambitious book, *The Far Lands*, and to produce enough of his autobiography for it to be published posthumously. There was also a book-length satirical poem, *A Word for His Sponsor*, and a collection of sketches and essays, *The Forgotten One and Other True Tales of the South Seas*, which was printed after his death as was a volume of commemorative birthday verses he had written for his daughter.

130 						JAMES NORMAN HALL

I *Apocalypse*

The earliest of these, *A Word for His Sponsor* (1949), is hardly a
cheerful work. The climactic event is nothing less than a nuclear
holocaust, albeit it occurs only in the protagonist's imagination. But
even without that disaster, the modern world as Hall depicts it is a
grim enough place. The superpowers, having barely survived a recent war, now seem teetering on the brink of an even more lethal
conflict. Russia is befouling the globe with lies and immobilizing
the United Nations with vetoes. Both the United States and the
Soviet Union are menacing nature and mankind by developing ever
more destructive atomic devices and by experimenting with germ
warfare. Already, innocent societies are being destroyed, for in the
South Pacific Bikini Island has been the site of an American bomb
test. Back in the United States labor conflicts are wrecking the
economy, cities are becoming overcrowded, and nature is being
defiled.

Depressed by the ghastly stories he must report each evening, the
central character in Hall's poem, Chester White, is a newscaster
who, in a wish-fulfilling dream, walks out of his studio in the middle
of a broadcast. Off he goes to a bench in a nearby park where the
litter and the stench of carbon monoxide do little to lift his spirits.
In quick succession he encounters Mrs. Bentley, wife of his sponsor;
a tramp named Uncle Sos (Samuel Oliver Saver); and his fiancée,
Helen. All three agree the world is in a mess and in their colloquy
denounce most aspects of contemporary society. As anyone who has
read much of Hall would anticipate, they place most of the blame
upon technology and upon the scientists, industrialists, and
politicians who control it. When Mrs. Bentley at one point says that
machines enabled the United States to save Europe from the Nazis,
White replies scornfully:

> Europe's hideous plight
> And world-wide death and desolation might
> Never have been, except for those who dreamed
> And built those engines.[1]

He proceeds to observe that technology enabled both sides in the
war to convert Europe into a charnel house.

They all go to a housing development site where work has been
halted on White's house by a labor-management squabble. After

Uncle Sos denounces both sides for their greed, the group accepts his offer to visit his shack near the city dump. There, in the midst of a veritable inferno—which symbolizes all the waste, ugliness, and unwholesomeness of modern industrial civilization—Sos has built an agreeable refuge for himself, supplying his abode with furnishings, books, and phonograph records salvaged from the refuse heaps. There, too, he has a volume of poems written by Ben Young, whom we would have little trouble in identifying with Hall even if Hall had not told us so in the Preface. More denunciations of the modern world follow—of its literature, its violence, its materialism. Finally, while White is sleeping, nuclear Armageddon occurs. He awakes to find the country outside contorted into a nightmare terrain. Soon survivors straggle in, among them Mr. Bentley and Ben Young, the wandering poet. The latter shows White an updated version of Tennyson's "Locksley Hall," narrated in 1941 by the grandson of Tennyson's hero. What emerges is a picture of England devastated in a world in which a young man's fancy turns to thoughts not of love but of death and hate.

Hall mitigates the bleakness of this fantasy by having White awake from it to learn that work is being resumed on his house, but he hardly negates that bleakness with such a conclusion. It may be argued, however, that the use of this hoary dream device is still an evasion. Why, we might ask, not have Chester really walk out of his studio in protest? Why not have the world really blow up? And why not have the work end with Ben Young's bitter parody of Tennyson, a fitting epitaph for the century which had succeeded Tennyson's century? The probable answer is that, although Hall had been distressed by the events of the 1940s, he refused to let them drive him to despair. The world would endure. And not merely would it survive, but, despite mankind's recent follies and crimes, and despite the pell-mell rate of growth, it would preserve some measure of continuity as represented by Chester and Helen's marriage and by their determination to get their house built.

The happy ending, moreover, is not the non sequitur a plot summary can make it seem. Despite its prevailing gloom, *A Word for His Sponsor* contains flickers of light which presage a favorable outcome. For one thing Hall's benign humor is seldom long absent. More important, his philosophy, which tinges even the darkest portions of the work, may not preclude a holocaust, but it makes one unlikely. The outrages of the twentieth century had distressed Hall but had not turned him against either mankind or nature. Furthermore he still would not concede that an irreconcilable schism existed between the two.

How, then, if man is good and nature is benign, had so much gone so amiss in such a short period of time? In *A Word for His Sponsor* Hall advances two hypotheses. One is a variant of the populism rife on the prairie during Hall's boyhood. The other presupposes that there are enough morally flawed persons at all levels of society to insure the existence of evil even though most people are well meaning.

The first of these propositions—that the ills of modern times are the doing mainly of elites—is articulated principally by Mrs. Bentley, who ironically is the wife of a millionaire industrialist. The brunt of her criticism, though, falls upon scientists and upon powerful figures in government and commerce who ravage the earth with the devices technology has given them. The real trouble with the "giants of the realm of Mind," she contends, is that they have lost the "common wisdom common folk possess" (12) and have forgotten "human love for Mother Earth that we have never lost, we common folk" (103).

Generally, her auditors agree with her sentiments, as presumably Hall himself does. Certainly neither Hall nor the other characters in this poem approve of the destructive machines modern science has wrought nor the use to which governments and industry have put them. Yet there are elements in this work, as well as in his other writings, to indicate that he was not simplistic enough to attribute the ills of his era exclusively to technology and its minions. When Uncle Sos observes that times are always out of joint, and that there are devils among the common folk as well as among the rich and powerful, he speaks for Hall or, at any rate, for that side of Hall which drew him to Conrad, Melville, and Francis Thompson. Hall had never denied that pain, death, and evil are facts of human existence; and his admiration for the authors who could courageously confront such realities was boundless.

What he did deny, however, as he denies it in this work, is that humanity as a species is vile or that nature is inimical to human weal. In fact, the individual characters in the poem are without exception decent and generous, and these characters span the social and economic spectrum from the wealthy Bentleys to the impecunious Uncle Sos. Nature fares no less well at Hall's hand. Aside from the praises he sings it through the pen of Ben Young, he depicts it as a self-renewing force which, after the nuclear blast, un-

dergoes an upheaval to cleanse itself of the "obscene and shameful
human wreckage" in order to "make room for the bath/Of beauty
once again" (87).

But despite the happy ending, the flickers of humor, and the
benign portrayal of individual people and of nature, *A Word for His
Sponsor* is disquieting in a way that the works he wrote before
World War II never are. The reason is not that new conditions had
compelled him to abandon his earlier values but that in the wake of
the latest conflict the world seemed even less hospitable to those
values than it had seemed before. In the interwar years technology
and commerce had appeared to menace mainly beauty and tranquility. After Hiroshima the very existence of the race had become
imperiled. And, even though Hall in this poem rejected the
likelihood of humanity's extinction, he still had to confront the fact
that urbanization with its consequent defilement of earth, air, and
water, was progressing even more rapidly than he had feared.

In *A Word for His Sponsor* Hall, nevertheless, offers us his old
ideals—art, individualism, solitude, and resignation. But the reflective individualist here, Uncle Sos, lives not on a lovely tropical isle
but in a city dump, gouging out a tiny crevice of beauty amidst
seemingly endless ugliness. As for Helen and Chester, they will live
on, presumably sustained by hope. But, meanwhile, their new
house will add to the suburban sprawl which offends them. The
best any of them can do is listen to Mozart, read the old masters,
and keep alive in their hearts Hall's vision of an idyllic, turn-of-the-
century Iowa compounded with South Sea vistas—a vision he expresses in lines he attributes to Ben Young:

> The G-Note Road that runs from my home town
> First south, then west: a phantom road; my own;
> Recalling dreams, when I have travelled there,
> . . . .
> Thinking of all Dvořák means to me,
> And, most of all, his New World Symphony
> During these latter days of man-made ill.
> Wind-ripples moving up a grassy hill.
> To see wind-darkened water from a ship
> Seven days becalmed; to feel her stir and slip
> Quietly on again, with gentle motion,
> Through "moonlit solitude of the midmost ocean" (78).

This passage is, of course, pure Hall. The road referred to at the outset was an actual thoroughfare which in Hall's boyhood years ran from Colfax out into the country and which he associated with the G-note just below middle C on his mother's piano. Here, as in so many of his works, he merges pre-World War I Iowa with the South Pacific and identifies both with works of art, in this case Dvořák's music and the phrase by Matthew Arnold quoted in the final line.

That this poem-within-a poem, entitled "Well-Loved Things," should be designated as being "after Rupert Brooke's 'The Great Lover' " is apposite. Not only was Brooke, author of "Tiare Tahiti," a devotee of the South Seas, but as a young, handsome, cultivated, gifted figure who died in the First World War, he became emblematic of the wasted youth, the betrayed promise, and the destruction of genteel civilization which have characterized this deadly century. The somewhat old fashioned Edwardian cast of his verse, moreover, makes it an apt model for Ben Young, an advocate of yesterday's values, just as later the manner of Tennyson is ironically appropriate for Young's anguished portrait of Britain's be-ing ravaged in 1941. Hall uses these poetic intonations from the past as a protest against modernity just as he uses generally throughout *A Word for His Sponsor* that most traditional of forms, pentameter couplets. The deliberate anachronism of mid-twentieth-century dialogue being conveyed through a Chaucerian verse pattern is less jarring than one might suppose. By and large Hall maintains a steady colloquial flow by using frequent enjambment, normal speech rhythms, and by keeping metaphors at a minimum. The result may not always be "poetic" as the term is understood by exegetes. But the verses carry along his narrative and luminously communicate whatever he wishes to express—heinous sins, no doubt, in some critical circles. But such sins can surely be pardoned in an author who says as much as Hall does in *A Word for His Sponsor*.

II   *The Past Invented*

If Hall had written nothing during his final years except *A Word for His Sponsor* and *The Far Lands*, his career would seem to betoken a progressive disenchantment with reality. The straight-forward autobiography and reportage of his first two books, after all, had led to his idealized travel sketches and reminiscences of the 1920s and the adventure fiction of the 1930s which had been succeeded by the melancholy fantasies of the late 1940s and early 1950s. Unfortunately the tidiness of the pattern is marred by the fact that he began work on his memoirs in 1948, and in 1949 produced a long sketch in his earlier manner about his recently deceased friend, Robert Dean Frisbie.

Yet, although Hall was protean enough to elude such rigid classifications, his last novel, *The Far Lands*, despite its utilization of Polynesian history, is as much as fantasy as *A Word for His Sponsor*. To be sure, Hall strove to be faithful to the known facts about ancient Polynesian life. But no less an authority than Peter Buck, the noted Maori anthropologist, then the director of the Bishop Museum in Honolulu, personally assured Hall that few incontrovertible specifics of the kind Hall sought had been discovered. Buck, furthermore, urged him to trust his imagination—advice he readily heeded.

Setting his story in a distant, myth-enshrouded past, Hall tells of the efforts of Maui, a Tongan prince dedicated to the worship of a peace-loving god, Tané, to lead his people away from the island of Kurapo, whose inhabitants were votaries of the war god Koro. The obvious parallel here to Moses and the injection of a love affair between Maui and the Koro-worshiping chief's daughter, Hina, make *The Far Lands* seem more a combination of the Book of Exodus and *Romeo and Juliet* than an authentic recreation of Polynesian legends. Then, too, the hidden cave in which Maui and Hina secretly meet and the presence of a villainous priest of Koro are more reminiscent of the novels Hall had written with Nordhoff than they are suggestive of folk epics.

Actually Nordhoff had warned Hall that the writing of such a book would be an "impossible task." Hall in retrospect conceded that his friend had been right, but added: "I failed, of course, but I have at least this satisfaction: if I were to try again, half a dozen times over, I don't believe I could have bettered it."[2] He should have had another satisfaction—or at least a consolation: even Herman Melville, that peerless transformer of ships and whales into cosmic symbols, had lapsed into frilly sentimentality and portentous tedium when he misdirected his genius to a South Sea never-never land in *Mardi*. After all, to set a novel, which requires a high degree of specificity if it is to come to life, in an utterly alien milieu about which few facts are available, creates well-nigh insurmountable problems.

Not the least of these problems is to devise a suitable style. In the

Bounty trilogy, *Botany Bay*, and *Doctor Dogbody's Leg* Hall had
used language which conveys a sense of the eighteenth century
without slavishly imitating the diction and syntax of that period.
But in those books he had been dealing with English-speaking
characters in a not-too-remote era. In *The Far Lands*, however,
Hall's attempts from time to time to affect a primitive epic style
only clash with the twentieth-century idiom which characterizes the
work as a whole. Thus the opening sentence—"I tell the story of our
ancestors of the Tongan clan from the time when they reached the
land of Kurapo"[3]—promises a type of language Hall does not fulfill
and probably could not have fulfilled, working as he was in a genre,
the novel, which requires a measure of verisimilitude incompatible
with the artificial cadences of the epic or the saga. Furthermore, the
injection throughout of bardic phrases such as "the story tells of a
day" and "now is told the manner in which the story progressed"
(16, 68) disconcerts us rather than persuades us we are reading an
authentic Polynesian saga. What makes these archaisms especially
incongruous is that they are being narrated not by a Tongan bard
but by a twentieth-century half-caste, Captain Winnie Brander,
who prefaces his story by warning: "You are not to question me too
closely as to how I succeeded in piecing together the fragments of
legend and folklore to make a connected tale of them" (xix).

The remarkable thing is that, while venturing in *The Far Lands*
into such deep water, Hall sometimes sank but never drowned.
Despite incongruities of plot and style, he was kept afloat much of
the time by the sheer exertion of imaginative effort. The world he
conjures up may lack the grandeur of myth and may seem too contemporary to strike us as a genuine recreation of a distant age. But
the actions, people, and places he depicts are all vivid enough to
make us suspend disbelief. Furthermore the book treats themes of
sufficient importance to keep it from seeming mere escapism.

Here, as in *Lost Island* and *A Word for His Sponsor*, Hall examines the subject of war versus peace. Yet, in *The Far Lands* even
more than in *Lost Island*, the optimism once proclaimed so
bouyantly is offered to the reader almost timidly. The follies of the
1920s and 1930s, after all, had been precisely that—follies. In
neither the growing industrialization of America nor the Depression
had he found evidence of human viciousness. As for World War I,
although he often attested to the disillusionment it had produced in
him, he continued to regard it as a great adventure—so great that in
Faery Lands of the South Seas he commented, without a tinge of

irony: "Had we been contemporaries and fellow explorers with De Quires, or Cook, or Bougainville we should have missed the Great War" (8).

The Second World War, however, merely appalled him. It was not, like its predecessor, a terrible yet somehow romantic blunder; it was the result of naked, predatory aggression. And, as he made amply clear in *Lost Island,* he recognized that the cold-blooded crimes of Germany and Japan had led the enemies of those nations to sin in turn against inoffensive peoples like his beloved Polynesians.

Although Hall states in the prologue to *The Far Lands* that the story of Maui's quest for the isles of peace was told to him by Captain Brander shortly after World War I, the tone of the story itself as well as of the prologue, epilogue, and the appended account of the legend of Maui-the-Peaceful accords much more with that of *Lost Island* than with the tone of anything Hall wrote in the 1920s or 1930s. Then, while dismayed by the materialism and philistinism of Western civilization, he had found nothing to make him doubt the basic goodness of most men. Even the Germans had treated him well as a prisoner of war. As for the virtues Europe and America seemed to lack—gentleness, tranquility, social and economic cooperation—these he had found in the South Seas. *Lost Island* reveals that World War II brought home to him the extent to which the viciousness and destructiveness of man can reach. In *The Far Lands,* glancing back at the remote past of his harmless, happy Polynesians, he finds himself forced to admit that even they were partial to violence. Speaking through Captain Brander, he can say no better of them than that they were less addicted to wholesale slaughter than are the nations of the twentieth century. And, in answer to the question of whether the Polynesians were lovers of peace, Brander can only reply lamely: "In every age there have been men who loathed war" (xviii - xix). The story that he then proceeds to relate about Maui, the seeker of peace, is, he admits, something he has pieced together from fragments of legend. The heart of the book, therefore, is not so much a reconstruction of the past as an act of faith on Hall's part—a mammoth assertion that at least one tribe of Polynesians *must* have shared his values, dreamed his dreams, and pursued his aspirations.

But, to Hall's question as to whether Koro, the god of war, eventually overtook Maui and his followers, Brander rejoins rhetorically: "Which power has triumphed down the ages? Tané, the God of

Peace, or Koro, the God of War?'' (272). To support his point, Brander observes that some Polynesians believe the famous stone images on Easter Island to be exact replicas of the statue of Koro "that Maui sent crashing down from the temple on Kurapo" (273). The haven sought and ultimately reached by Maui and his Tongans, consequently, turns out to be no haven at all. Just as war had come to Hall's own island world, so, centuries before, it had come to one of the most isolated places in the Pacific Ocean.

Despite history, despite legend, and despite his own experiences and those of his contemporaries, Hall refused in this, his final novel, to succumb to pessimism. Are there no real havens? Well, there are, he asserts, ideal ones. Returning to a theme he and Nordhoff had stated twenty-nine years earlier in the preface to their first volume on Polynesia, *Faery Lands of the South Seas,* Hall concludes his career in *The Far Lands,* as he had begun it, by celebrating tranquility, reverie, and imagination. Maui, the seeker of an earthly Eden and thus a Polynesian prototype of the modern Utopian, may be the hero of the novel, but his quest is ultimately a failure. For Hall, the character who embodies the only course leading to contentment is Tavi, a demigod who emerges from *The Far Lands* as a combination of Plato, Keats, and James Norman Hall. "A creator of beauty in ideal form" (230), Tavi is also the laziest of the demigods. Too indolent to fish real islands from the sea like his older brothers, Mano and Tumu, he prefers to shape phantom lands that can never be reached but which are eternal. At the end of the epilogue, rejecting Brander's pessimistic contention that the god of war must always prevail, Hall asserts: "I said nothing to Winnie, but I was thinking of images more enduring than stone: the Phantom Lands of Tavi, miscalled 'the Jester.' . . . An idealist, yes, but I have enough faith in humankind to believe that a time will come when his Phantom Lands will no longer fade into empty sea and empty sky before the eyes of men" (273). Thus, although Hall in 1950 may have been a sadder man than when he arrived in Polynesia thirty years before, he was still not a defeated one.

III   *Posthumous Works*

On Friday, July 6, 1951, in his home in Arué overlooking Matavai Bay where the *Bounty* had dropped anchor, James Norman Hall died. Although the end came swiftly, he had not been unprepared because in the preceding year he had learned from doctors in

Boston that he was suffering from a serious coronary ailment. His response was a characteristic blend of courage, equanimity, and recklessness. Back he went to Tahiti, where he worked on his autobiography. But, for all his love of life, he refused to cling to it in the craven manner that now seems the norm: thus he gave up neither smoking nor his usually moderate drinking. Neither did he persist in the elaborate exercises prescribed for him.

By all accounts one of the most beloved men ever to have resided in Tahiti, he was mourned by numerous people of all degrees, native and white. Yet, though he was being interred on an island in the South Pacific, there were reminders of the birthplace which had never been long out of his thoughts. As his body was being borne to its hearse, a phonograph intoned his favorite piece of music, the Largo from the *New World Symphony*, which he was convinced Dvořák had composed during his sojourn in Iowa. And on his tombstone was inscribed a quatrain he had written half a century earlier in Colfax.

In the year after his death, 1952, three works of his were published: *Her Daddy's Best Ice Cream, The Forgotten One and Other True Tales of the South Seas*, and *My Island Home*. The first of these, a volume of verses commemorating the birthdays of his daughter, need not concern us. Printed privately in Honolulu, it is too personal in its tone, too much a memento of a father's affection for his child and of his desire to amuse her with allusions to their own small world to lend itself to the kind of scrutiny required in a study of this nature.

As for *The Forgotten One*, four of its selections—the title story, "Captain Handy's Memoirs," "Sing: A Song of Sixpence," and "A Happy Hedonist"—appeared earlier in either *On the Stream of Travel* (1926) or *Mid-Pacific* (1928); consequently, we have already discussed them. We should note, however, that "Captain Handy's Memoirs" had initially been part of a selection entitled "Occupation: Journalist" and that "The Forgotten One" here concludes with material from a 1931 article about Crichton's death, "Death on an Atoll."[4] In the latter, Hall reveals that Crichton had fled into exile on a remote island because of anguish over his homosexuality. The revelation, to be sure, divests Crichton of some of the grandeur he had possessed when his pathological craving for solitude had seemed motivated by an ill-defined *Weltschmerz*. Yet, when Hall was summoned to the Tuamotus by Arthur Cridland, the real-life prototype for Crichton, to learn the truth from the lips of the dying man, it was inevitable that he would write an account of the experience and equally inevitable that the new work would be appended to any reprinting of the earlier story.

This volume, however, contains two pieces written during Hall's last years—"Rivnac" and "Frisbie of Danger Island." "Rivnac," much the shorter of the two, perfectly exemplifies two major themes of this study: Hall's profound attachment to the Iowa of his youth and his penchant for injecting Iowa into works set in the South Pacific. For that matter, most of Hall's other preoccupations are also present: his distrust of technology, his disdain for "progress," his disapproval of recent fashions in the arts, his detestation of modern warfare, his fondness for leisure and solitude, and his belief in the transfiguring power of art and imagination.

The focal point for all this is a Czech hotel proprietor in Tahiti who shared Hall's enthusiasm for Dvořák. Over the years, starting in 1927, they would reminisce, listen to music, philosophize, and, after the rise of Hitler, discuss the ominous course of events in Europe. During World War II, after Rivnac's homeland was occupied by the Germans, Hall returned to Tahiti from a visit to the United States with a new recording of the *New World Symphony* as a gift for his friend. Rivnac, though, had died. To mourn him, Hall and the native woman who worked at the hotel played recordings of Dvořák's *Slavonic Dances*.

In "Rivnac" Hall is explicit about what Dvořák's music represented to him—late nineteenth-century Iowa and its lost values. Once while bicycling in Tahiti, he assures us, the sound of the *New World Symphony* from Rivnac's place caused the scenery around him to vanish: "in the imagination, I was again walking northward along a country road in Iowa."[5] This association, he insists, was not arbitrary. He was convinced, despite contentions of some critics to the contrary, that Dvořák had composed the score during his sojourn in Spillville, Iowa.

What makes "Rivnac," like so many of Hall's later works, poignant is the sense it conveys of his awareness of the chasm between his own late nineteenth-century vision of mankind's potentialities (here identified with Dvořák's music) and the barbarities of the twentieth century. The poignancy is heightened here by indications that, while his faith in the value of that vision had not waned, he recognized to a greater measure than hitherto the dangers of becoming totally absorbed by it. His remark that "Tahiti comes nearest to being the earthly counterpart of Tennyson's Land of the

Lotos-Eaters" (133) may seem a not particularly noteworthy instance of Hall's South Sea exoticism. But the statement acquires in retrospect a darker cast when he later observes: "I need not remind the reader of the Evil growing to monstrous proportions during the years 1937 - 1939; and how the leaders of great nations might have been kings among the lotos-eaters" (146). Hall, furthermore, confesses that those leaders were not alone in ignoring political perils because he himself during the 1920s and 1930s did not own a radio. He acknowledges that he was "something of a human ostrich" (143), though one with his head "in the clouds, not buried in the sand." As "a firm believer in the fundamental decency of human beings . . . with a deep faith in mankind's inherited, collective wisdom," he had found it inconceivable that a man like Hitler could come to power in the homeland of so many great composers and poets—and of his own beloved Professor Shreve of Grinnell, who had introduced Hall to Dvořák's music (144). But the inconceivable had occurred. Thus, in the inferno that the mid-twentieth century had become, nightmares seemed closer to reality than the old Iowa-bred dreams did. Still, those dreams must not be abandoned. And they would not be, at least by Hall, as long as works of art like Dvořák's music endured or as long as his memories of Iowa and of people like Rivnac could keep them alive.

The one serious blemish in this moving work is its final paragraph. There sentiment gives way to sentimentality. Not content with closing with the scene at the hotel during which he and Henrietta play Rivnac's favorite records, Hall insists upon conjuring up the shade of his departed friend and upon having him trudge along a country road in "the last faint light of evening" (153). This is a literary equivalent of those dreadful endings of 1930s movies, such as *Gunga Din* and *Three Comrades*, in which the superimposed image of a deceased character grins out at the audience or marches off into the dusk with his living friends.

A similar conclusion tarnishes "Frisbie of Danger Island," the longest selection in the book and, apart from its ending, one of the best things Hall ever wrote. To be sure, he had a well-nigh perfect subject in his late friend, Robert Dean Frisbie. Compared to Frisbie, most writers, great or small, have led drab lives. How many of them have lived through a hurricane, clinging to a palm tree buffeted by raging winds and slashed by giant waves? How many have suffered from elephantiasis, wandered about the mid-Pacific bringing up a brood of half-Polynesian children, or have been for many years the sole white resident on a remote atoll rarely visited by even the smallest ship?

But Hall does more than record the fascinating outline of Frisbie's tragic life. By drawing upon Frisbie's letters to him as well as upon personal recollections, he provides a vivid character portrait of his flamboyant friend. Here, no less than in his own books, Frisbie blazes forth in all his splendid contradictions—irascible one moment, gentle the next, always articulate, frequently impious yet fundamentally religious, and occasionally violent. Here we see the man who with almost suicidal frenzy threw himself into the life of Polynesia, ceaselessly seeking an ever more complete isolation from what he regarded as the harassments of twentieth-century civilization. Yet, as his letters to Hall reveal, the greater his isolation and the more serene the outward circumstances of his existence, the more dissatisfied with the world and himself he became. One moment he was proclaiming himself a Buddhist; the next he was ranting like a South Sea Nietzsche. Although for nearly three decades he insisted that only in Polynesia could he find happiness, his letters from Puka Puka, as well as those from Samoa, Rarotonga, and Manihiki abound in complaints. It must be admitted, however, that he had much to complain about. If life in the islands cured or arrested the tuberculosis he had when he arrived there, that life brought other varieties of ill health, did nothing to assuage his thirst for alcohol, nudged him into the use of narcotics, and, for all the beauty and charm of his books, failed to inspire him to become the great writer he aspired to be.

It should be obvious why the two men were such close friends. To be sure, nearly everybody who got to know Hall liked him. But in all the wide Pacific there must have been no man who shared as many of Hall's preferences and antipathies as Frisbie did. Both adored Polynesia and loved books. Both longed for solitude yet craved companionship. Both were given to reverie and introspection. Both had a mystical strain and at the same time eschewed formal religion. Both disliked technology, commerce, urban life.

But there was this major difference between them: Frisbie was an extremist; Hall was not. What Hall merely dreamed about or practiced moderately, Frisbie flung himself into with abandonment. Thus, whereas Hall's yearning for solitude would find its outlet in afternoon strolls through the interior of Tahiti or in abortive "adventures in solitude" on other islands, Frisbie would sequester himself for long periods of time in lonely places and once sailed off with his children to the uninhabited island of Suvarrow, where he intended to remain for the rest of his life. Hall, residing on one of the less primitive islands in the South Pacific, would make brief visits to remote atolls. Frisbie lived on such an atoll, Puka Puka, from the late 1920s until the early 1940s, where, as the only white man in the place, he married two native women (consecutively, not conjointly) and fathered seven children. Hall's primitivism, as we have seen, was partial and intermittent. Frisbie's was unbounded. As Hall says: "Whenever he spoke of 'civilization' he placed unseen quotation marks around the word" (160). Even as a writer he lacked Hall's restraint. Thus the autobiographical mode, which enabled Hall to make himself a focal point as he depicted the world about him, became for Frisbie at one point an obsessive solipsism. Once he told Hall that he aspired to have a single subject: himself. Hall was incredulous: "I was astonished . . . to hear this twenty-one year old talk so confidently of a task in which no one, however honest, however gifted, could hope to succeed" (157).

Any work as personal as this essay inevitably reveals as much about its author as about its subject. The very tone of the writing reflects those qualities which Frisbie undoubtedly most liked about Hall—sympathy, good humor, tolerance, common sense, and, yes, sanity. Hall's affection for Frisbie emanates from every paragraph. So too does his approval of many of Frisbie's aspirations and beliefs. Yet he manages to indicate disapproval of his friend's intemperance without sounding self-righteously censorious. There was, of course, a bit of the Puritan in Hall—a fact both men recognized and joked about. But that tinge of puritanism never drove him to try to reform his friend as a certain professor in Papeete once did with unfortunate results. For one thing, Hall was wise enough to realize that such attempts were apt to bring forth "the reckless, defiant Frisbie who could not and would not be lectured to" (161). For another, Hall was too much the individualist to tamper with the individuality of others. If Frisbie intoxicated became "a braggart and a boaster," Hall's response was the simple and sensible one of avoiding him whenever he was in that condition.

Sermons were not Hall's style. In fact, he apparently conversed with friends in the same civil and considerate manner in which he addressed his readers. No wonder so many people loved him. No wonder, too, that he has lost readers in an era in which the favorite mode of literary discourse seems to be the harangue.

IV *Home Again*

Despite its title, Hall's autobiography tells us comparatively little about his life in the South Seas, and much of that he had told us in earlier writings. Of *My Island Home*'s 360 pages, a mere sixty-two are devoted to Polynesia, and twenty-six of those reproduce portions of *Faery Lands of the South Seas* (1920) and *Under a Thatched Roof* (1942). Similar borrowings inflate the lengthy segment devoted to Hall's wartime experiences and the briefer section about his Iceland sojourn. The most informative, moving, and original portions are those pertaining to Hall's youth in Iowa, his early manhood in Boston, and his return to his native state the year before his death.

But we must not see in the superiority of these pages (as one anonymous reviewer did) evidence that Hall might have been a better writer if he had remained in the United States.[6] After all, the Iowa and Boston chapters were written to serve the fuction they perform here and are obviously in a finished or nearly finished state. Much of the material elsewhere, however, is a patchwork of old and new. No doubt some of its inchoate quality would have been eliminated if Hall had lived long enough to revise his work more extensively and to fill in certain gaps he had left in it.

Then, too, as we have frequently noted, Hall had never for long ceased thinking about Iowa—or for long ceased writing about it, because throughout his career he had devoted numerous sketches and essays to it. But his depiction of Iowa in those earlier selections differs substantially from his treatment of it in *My Island Home*. In the former he tends to conjure up his boyhood milieu in impressionistic snippets. He also changes names and heightens incidents in the manner of the writer of fiction. Furthermore, he often juxtaposes pre-World War I Iowa with the present either to contrast it with a later, machine-ravaged America or to suggest analogies between it and Polynesia. In *My Island Home*, on the other hand, he offers a sustained account of his youthful years in Colfax and Grinnell, giving people and places their actual names. This is not to say this picture of the past is any more "true," in the profoundest sense, than the ones he offers in, say, "One Kind of Journey" or "A Middle Western School." What is more, that picture may actually reveal less about Hall's own real attitude toward Colfax than the verses in *Oh Millersville!* do. Nowhere else, however, does he communicate his affections for late nineteenth-century and early twentieth-century Iowa in such detail and so vividly as in *My Island Home*.

It is highly unlikely (whatever the above-mentioned reviewer might have suggested to the contrary) that Hall could have written these pages if he had remained at home. What gives them their glow is the sense Hall communicates in them of recalling a lost world. The tone is elegiac, the vision that of a man describing sights and events from which he is separated by an impenetrable barrier. Actually, there are two barriers—space and time. Together they give him the kind of distance from his subject matter that cultural differences had provided when he was writing about the Tuamotu Archipelago. As a result, the Iowa chapters are reminiscent of his travel sketches, for in both he combines an anecdotal, discursive presentation with an affectionate, detached manner.

In the final chapter of *My Island Home*, Hall reveals what happened when one of the barriers separating him from Iowa was eliminated—space. As Edward Weeks suggests, Hall, probably realizing that his end was imminent, wrote an appropriate conclusion for his book even though he had not yet finished other portions. Near the beginning of this concluding chapter he assures us: "Iowa, for all the years I have been away from it, has always been, and still is, home to me."[7] Furthermore, he informs us he has maintained a link with his past by corresponding with old friends and classmates.

Yet, in these pages in which he bids farewell not just to Colfax but to the earth, Hall never becomes maudlin. Back home he discovers that reality has betrayed his expectations. Unlike Nordhoff, who had believed that a person should never return to a place where he had known happiness, Hall had contended that "happy memories could never be destroyed by a return to the old haunts concerned with them." But when Hall discovers that a giant V-shaped cut has been made right through his favorite hill, "which held so many happy associations connected with boyhood and youth," he realizes that he has "returned once too often" (340).

But, however much this realization may sadden him, it does not make him despair. Technology may have vandalized a cherished place of natural beauty; it cannot expunge the beauty from his mind: "Nevertheless, I still have it from memory. . . . The stench of burned Diesel oil from all the Rock Island trains that pass and are yet to pass through it can never destroy, for me, the fragrance of the hepaticas that once grew on its slopes" (341).

Proof of how potent his memory of the old Iowa was lies in the opening chapters of *My Island Home*. There his beloved hill is restored, old men recapture their youth, the G-note road regains its pastoral lure, the odious automobile becomes merely a future menace, and war seems only a romantic possibility. But even as this Iowa recedes from our attention when Hall takes us with him to the slums of Boston, the trenches and aerial combats of France, to New York, Iceland, and the South Pacific, it seldom disappears for long even though it may be present only as a half-recollected vision of a peaceful and humane world in an era becoming ever more violent and inhuman.

In *My Island Home* Hall's memory is, of course, selective. It passes over the boredom, the parochialism, the pettiness, the philistinism, and the intolerance that have too often characterized life in the back reaches of America. Perhaps, despite the specificity of his reminiscences about Colfax and Grinnell, he should have prefaced the opening section of his book with a warning similar to the one he gave his readers about the Tuamotu Archipelago in the first chapter of *Faery Lands of the South Seas*: "But one can't be wholly matter of fact in writing about these islands. They are not real in the ordinary sense, but belong rather, to the realm of the imagination" (9). But discerning readers should not require such a warning. As they read through *My Island Home*, they will soon enough realize that the lens attached to Hall's soul enabled him to see acutely what was best in turn-of-the-century Iowa as well as in Polynesia and also to perceive that the virtues of those places were woefully absent from modern urbanized Europe and America. Such a vision may not have embraced the entire truth about the twentieth century, but it encompassed a truth broad enough to merit our attention and our respect.

CHAPTER 11

Hall: Past, Present, and Future

H ALL has been a rare and perhaps unparalled phenomenon in American literature. For the last two decades of his life he was one of the best-known writers in the English-speaking world. Not only did the romances he wrote with Nordhoff sell well; so did his solo achievements as a novelist. Moreover, for more than three decades he was a steady contributor to a respected journal, the *Atlantic*, and a frequent one to the *Atlantic*'s peer and rival, *Harper's*. No mere popular entertainer, he wrote in almost every genre, was never less than a skilled craftsman, and often dealt with important subjects in an effective manner. His works were nearly always favorably reviewed. Although his popularity undoubtedly has declined since his death, the *Bounty* trilogy has remained constantly in print, usually in competing editions, and other books of his, both fiction and nonfiction, have always been readily available. Moreover, in the 1960s he and Nordhoff were the subject of a dual biography by Paul L. Briand, Jr., and Hall himself was the focal point of Leland Johnson's *The American Heritage of James Norman Hall*. There have also been numerous shorter works about Hall, the man, the most noteworthy of which are cited in the bibliography. One would suppose, therefore, that so visible and prolific an author who has been accorded respect by the few people who have commented upon his works in print would have received substantial attention from scholars. The truth has been otherwise. Literary historians have ignored him. Academic journals, which in recent years have often found space for articles about far more obscure and less literate figures, have taken almost no cognizance of him. The only significant exception is an offering in the *South Atlantic Quarterly* in which the author, Murray D. Welsh, maintains, as does the author of this study, that Hall's essays are his most significant works.[1] A French scholar, Jean Simon, in a 1939 work, *La Polynésie dans l'art et la littérature de l'occident*, mentions Hall along with

Nordhoff but provides little more about them than bibliographical information.[2] The one substantial American scholarly book even to refer to Hall has been James Baird's *Ishmael: A Study in the Symbolic Mode of Primitivism*; Baird gives him short shrift in this study of Melville and Melville's literary progeny on the instructive grounds that Hall—like Nordhoff, Frisbie, and Maugham—"was devoted to narrative as the preëminent responsibility of art rather than to *poesis*," which he defines as "rendering symbolically the subjective and multiple."[3]

Baird's comment probably partially explains why Hall has been neglected—and, in the process, reveals as much about the predilections of academic critics as it does about Hall. Academicians sometimes may enjoy writers like Hall, but they do not "study" them. In truth, the bias of scholarly criticism is in favor of the obscure over the lucid, the complex over the simple. The reason is self-evident. "Difficult" authors lend themselves to interpretation more readily than straightforward ones like Hall do.

There is another reason why Hall has been slighted. Although he may not have been a symbolist or a contriver of unalloyed fantasies, he conveys the impression of having been something scholars find it difficult to take seriously—an escapist. His best-known novels can be dismissed, however unfairly, as mere melodrama, diverting but insubstantial. As for his less-familiar volumes of nonfiction, their very titles—*Under a Thatched Roof, Mid-Pacific, On the Stream of Travel*—are more likely to evoke contempt with their promise of warmed-over Melville and Loti than to arouse the curiosity of anyone seeking neglected masterpieces to dissect.

Hall, of course, was hardly alone among writers of his time in seeking refuge from the vexations of modern life. Many authors of the 1920s expatriated themselves or retreated into an agreeable fantasy land. Hall's choice of havens, though, no less than his aesthetic preferences, set him directly against some of the mightiest intellectual currents of the twentieth century—currents which may now be shifting in his favor. If there are two places incompatible with the values propounded by writers such as Eliot, Pound, and Stein, those places are a turn-of-the-century Midwestern village and a Polynesian island. But as a self-styled "reactionary old-fogey," Hall sought to perpetuate, in both life and art, norms and ideals which the "best minds" were most determined to demolish.

In 1950 Lionel Trilling commented upon the indifference to or hostility of modern European writers to the tradition of democratic liberals.[4] European authors were not alone in that antipathy toward democracy. Pound, Eliot, and Mencken on the right and numerous writers on the left in the 1930s were drawn to authoritarian societies.

Now, whatever they may have been in actuality, Polynesia and rural Iowa of the 1890s and 1900s emerge from Hall's pen as the antitheses of such places. It is not the violence of the recently vanished frontier that Hall stresses but the serenity and informal egalitarianism of the prairie village. The caste system of the South Seas that Bligh censured, Hall all but ignores as he usually ignores the cannibalism, human sacrifices, and perpetual warfare which were rife throughout the Pacific before the advent of the white man. Instead he concentrates on the peace, the leisurely pace of life, and the cohesion of communities in Polynesia.

Herein lies another problem for Hall. In an age in which the most esteemed writers from Joyce to Hemingway and from Eliot to Faulkner strove for a firmness of vision to match the hardness of their schemes of values, Hall was proclaiming himself a romantic idealist of a sort who would have been much more at ease with Shelley on the shores of Lake Geneva than he ever would have been at one of Gertrude Stein's gatherings in Paris. Indeed, it is easier to conceive of Eliot, Pound, or Hemingway having written "Ode to a Skylark" than to imagine any of them saying about a prospective literary subject as Hall said of the Tuamotu Archipelago islands in one of his chapters in *Faery Lands of the South Seas*: "They are not real in the ordinary sense, but belong, rather to the realm of the imagination. And it is only in the imagination that you can ever conceive of having been there" (9).

And so, is it any wonder that, however skillfully and conscientiously he wrote, however popular his books were, or whatever anyone may have said in their favor, "serious" critics refused to take him seriously? He was an idealist in an age that scorned idealism: a writer of popular romances in decades that venerated either grim realism or gnarled symbolism. He was a staunch traditionalist in an epoch of innovation, a devotee of Dvořák in a period that doted upon either the neoclassical or the ultramodern, a lotus-eater in a world overrun by roughnecks; a sane, wholesome man in a time when neurosis was in style; and a best-selling author when being popular meant being shallow and vulgar.

Much of this might not have mattered if Hall had written only fiction. The collaborative nature of the novels he wrote with

Nordhoff as well as their heavy reliance on plot contrivances resulted in an impersonality similar to that of Hollywood screenplays of the 1930s. Hall, to be sure, often injected his ideas into these works. But, just as an adamant anti-Marxist can often enjoy movies of the Depression era despite their left-wing "messages," so someone can respond favorably to *Mutiny on the Bounty* without being the least in sympathy with Hall's values. Those values are there, as we have seen. But Nordhoff's contributions dilute them, as do the imperatives of the genre. The problem with these books is not that their contents dissuade people from wanting to read them but that scholars have refused to take them at least as seriously as many film critics have learned to take once-disdained popular films of the past. This is not to say that *Mutiny on the Bounty* is not melodramatic or that *The Hurricane* is not contrived. But the adroit blending of childlike fantasy and solid historical reality in the former and the moral intensity of the latter more than counterbalance their defects. Despite their apparent simplicity, moreover, they are not devoid of subtleties, and even ambiguities.

The novels Hall wrote without Nordhoff, for all their felicities, do not represent him at his best. His predilection was for the brief sketch or essay, where his raconteur's flair for a relaxed tone, timely digressions, and for depicting a scene or person with a quick stroke served him well. In his longer works, without Nordhoff to restrain him, he often became diffuse and too overtly didactic. Furthermore, his characters are static and often ill-defined, and he was unable to find a wholly satisfactory point of view.

Hall's verse is usually pleasant and sometimes cogent, but minor. We cannot object, per se, to his use of traditional forms. After all, Robert Frost, one of Hall's idols, achieved superb results within such forms. Frost, however, was able to infuse traditional poetic modes with a new and distinctive character; Hall was not.

Where Hall is both distinctive and in complete control of his material is in his essays and sketches. There he fuses tone, form, and style perfectly with his themes. There, too, he succeeds in converting his own engaging personality into an effective persona—tolerant, inquiring, modest yet knowledgeable, idiosyncratic but sensible.

It is appropriate that most of these short nonfiction pieces should have appeared initially in periodicals, because they are specimens of journalism in the best sense of that often debased term. They are an intelligent, literate man's comments on the world about him, but comments designed "to resist obsessive concern with the here and now." Unfortunately there seems to be an *a priori* assumption, at least in this country, that such offerings go out of date after a few spins of the globe.

Then, too, since the essayist addresses himself far less obliquely to his subject than either the poet or the novelist does, we are less inclined to read him, whatever his merits, if we feel we are unlikely to care for what he says. Thus even that nonpareil of journalists, that master iconoclast, H. L. Mencken, suffered a precipitous decline in prestige and popularity during the 1930s when readers who had formerly been delighted by his attacks on the "great unwashed" and the "booboisie" found his writings at best beside the point despite their wit and their verbal acrobatics.

The time may have arrived, however, for us to begin turning to Hall, the essayist. His objections to progress and bigness—objections which might have seemed quaint during his lifetime and downright perverse during the forward-and-upward years of the Kennedy and Johnson administrations—foreshadowed the recent calls for zero population growth, a slowdown in industrial expansion, and for modes of living more in harmony with nature. His insistence upon the value of reverie, moreover, presaged the current fascination with various forms of meditation. And surely his belief that certain unspoiled areas of the globe should be kept unspoiled should appeal to members of the Sierra Club. Even his doting on Dvořák no longer seems misguided, as a glance at recent programs of major symphony orchestras and at record reviews in music magazines will confirm.

Yet, Hall's idiosyncratic traditionalism in the arts as well as in his philosophy could serve as a well-needed corrective to the faddishness that characterizes too many of the trends he anticipated. His humor and common sense, furthermore, are in refreshing contrast to the acerbity and hysteria that have marred so much public discourse in our day. Then, too, his essays have a virtue woefully lacking in many recent magazine offerings dealing with similar subjects: they are entertaining.

Hall does not harangue us. Neither does he offer us panaceas. Indeed, he would have been horrified if a substantial number of his readers had emulated him by emigrating to Tahiti—just as horrified as his hero, Thoreau, would have been if all the residents of Concord had built shacks in the environs of Walden Pond. But Hall—a more tolerant, resigned and less self-righteous man than

Thoreau—probably either would have made the best of things or would have moved quietly on to another island. And afterwards he would have written an essay about the incident, sad, faintly hopeful, and touched with humor as well as with wit. Hall was no early incarnation of William F. Buckley, with a self-appointed mission to stand in the roadway of history and exclaim "Halt!" He chose, instead, to sit in the shade by the roadside and urge those passersby not too hurried to listen to slow down and ask themselves whether they really wanted to go where the road was leading them.

Notes and References

Preface

1. Edmund Wilson, "T. S. Eliot and the Church of England," *The Shores of Light: A Literary Chronicle of the Twenties and Thirties* (New York, 1952), pp. 438 - 41.

2. The total is seventeen if the privately and posthumously published *Her Daddy's Best Ice Cream*, a volume of commemorative birthday verses for Hall's daughter, is included.

3. Ellery Sedgwick, "James Norman Hall," *Atlantic*, CLXXXVIII (September 1951), 21.

Chapter One

1. "Talk," *Under a Thatched Roof* (Boston, 1942), p. 20.

2. "A Small Dissenting Voice," *Under a Thatched Roof*, p. 80.

3. "Expatriates," *American Review*, V (May 1935), 190.

4. Robert Leland Johnson, *The American Heritage of James Norman Hall: The Woodshed Poet of Iowa and Co-Author of Mutiny on the Bounty* (Philadelphia, 1969), pp. xiii - xiv, 50.

5. *My Island Home: An Autobiography* (Boston, 1952), pp. 4 - 5. Subsequent quotations in Chapters One, Two, and Three pertaining to Hall's life will be from this edition of this work, unless there are indications to the contrary, and page numbers will be in parentheses.

6. *The Tale of a Shipwreck* (Boston, 1934), pp. 40 - 41.

7. "Iceland," *On the Stream of Travel* (Boston, 1926), p. 166.

8. "Why I Live in Tahiti," *On the Stream of Travel*, p. 87.

9. "Fifth Avenue in Fog," *Century*, LXXXVII (February 1914), 622; "Charwoman," *Bellman*, XVI (June 6, 1914), 713.

Chapter Two

1. Paul L. Briand, Jr., *In Search of Paradise: The Nordhoff-Hall Story* (New York, 1966), p. 121.

2. *Mid-Pacific* (Boston, 1928), pp. 213 - 32.

3. *Kitchener's Mob: The Adventures of an American in Kitchener's Army* (Boston, 1916), p. 68. Subsequent quotations, with page numbers in parentheses, are from this edition.

4. "Poetry Under the Fire Test," *New Republic*, IX (November 25, 1916), 93 - 96.

5. "The Unromantic English," *Outlook*, CXVI (July 18, 1917), 443 - 44.

Chapter Three

1. Hall's decorations included the *Croix de Guerre*, the *Légion d'Honneur*, the *Medaille Militaire*, and the Distinguished Service Cross.
2. *My Island Home*, pp. 201 - 202, n.
3. *High Adventure: A Narrative of Air Fighting in France* (Boston, 1918), p. 179. Subsequent quotations, with page numbers in parentheses, are from this edition.
4. *My Island Home*, p. 237.
5. *The Tale of a Shipwreck*, p. 11.

Chapter Four

1. Frederick O'Brien's *White Shadows in the South Seas* (New York, 1919) was on the best-seller list of *Publisher's Weekly* from April 1920 to July 1921.
2. Frederick O'Brien, review of *Faery Lands of the South Seas*, *New York Evening Post*, December 3, 1921, p. 226.
3. T. S. Eliot, "Byron," *On Poetry and Poets* (New York, 1961), p. 227.
4. *Faery Lands of the South Seas* (New York, 1921), p. 196. Subsequent quotations, with page numbers in parentheses, are from this edition.
5. "Occupation: Journalist," *Mid-Pacific*, p. 5.
6. "Tahiti's Coconut-Radio Service," *Mid-Pacific*, p. 265.
7. "Why I Live in Tahiti," *On the Stream of Travel*, p. 361.
8. In *The Forgotten One and Other True Tales of the South Seas* (Boston, 1952), pp. 3 - 51.
9. Edward Weeks, *In Friendly Candor* (Boston, 1959), p. 69.
10. Briand, pp. 303 - 309.
11. These details about Hall's marriage come from Horace Sutton's "Day on Bounty Bay," *Saturday Review of Literature*, XXXIX (July 14, 1956), 25 - 26.
12. Briand, p. 310.
13. Sutton, p. 25.
14. *My Island Home*, p. 300.
15. Arthur O. Lovejoy et al., eds., *A Documentary History of Primitivism and Related Ideas* (Baltimore, 1935).
16. "The Land Very Far Away," *Woman's Home Companion*, XLIX (November 1922), 11 - 12; "Some Polynesian Grandmothers," *Woman's Home Companion*, L (June 1923), 25.

Chapter Five

1. Edward Weeks is the principal source of information about the work methods of the team. Briand is also useful, as is James McConnaughey in "By Nordhoff and Hall," *Saturday Evening Post* CCX (April 23, 1938), 12, 13, 76, 78, 81, 82.

2. *Flying With Chaucer* (Boston, 1930), p. 15. Subsequent quotations, with page numbers in parentheses, are from this edition.

Chapter Six

1. *My Island Home*, p. 312.
2. *Ibid.*, p. 313.
3. Weeks, p. 350.
4. *Ibid.*
5. Ellery Sedgwick, *The Happy Profession* (Boston, 1946), p. 221.
6. *Mutiny on the Bounty* (Boston, 1932), p. 285. Subsequent quotations, with page numbers in parentheses, are from this edition.
7. [Sir John Barrow], *The Eventful History of the Mutiny and Piratical Seizure of the H. M. S. Bounty: Its Causes and Consequences* (London, 1831), pp. 178, 211.
8. "At Forty-Five," *Atlantic*, CL (September 1932), 356.
9. See Briand for a vivid and detailed account of Nordhoff's deterioration.
10. The manuscript at Grinnell College, however, contains a passage in the epilogue in which Byam as an old man goes to Pitcairn Island and learns from Alexander Smith about the events there. This subsequently deleted section, unlike the rest of the epilogue, was written on Hall's typewriter.
11. *Men Against the Sea* (Boston, 1934), p. 12. Subsequent quotations, with page numbers in parentheses, are from this edition.
12. Weeks, p. 78.
13. *Ibid.*
14. Harry L. Shapiro, *The Heritage of the Bounty: The Story of Pitcairn through Six Generations* (New York, 1936), p. 46.
15. F. W. Beechey, *Narrative of a Voyage to the Pacific and Beering* [sic] *Strait* (London, 1831), I, 80 - 85.
16. J. A. Shillibeer, *A Narrative of the Briton's Voyage to Pitcairn Island* (London, 1817), p. 85.
17. Folger reported his findings in a letter to the British Admiralty. The contents of the letter are quoted in Harry L. Shapiro's *Heritage of the Bounty*, pp. 49 - 51.
18. *Pitcairn's Island* (Boston, 1934), p. 30. Subsequent quotations, with page numbers in parentheses, are from this edition. Although the island is usually spelled "Pitcairn," Nordhoff and Hall's "Pitcairn's" follows earlier usage.
19. *The Tale of a Shipwreck* (Boston, 1934), pp. 35 - 41. Subsequent quotations, with page numbers in parentheses, are from this edition.

Chapter Seven

1. Review of *The Hurricane*, *Times Literary Supplement*, May 16, 1936, p. 418; Helen MacAfee, review of *The Hurricane*, *Yale Review*, XXV

(Spring 1936), viii; Lewis Garnett, review of *The Hurricane, New York Herald Tribune,* September 26, 1937, p. 21; Otis Ferguson, review of *The Hurricane, New Republic,* LXXXVI (March 18, 1936), 172.

2. *The Hurricane* (Boston, 1936), pp. 107, 110. Subsequent quotations, with page numbers in parentheses, are from this edition.

3. "Poetry Under the Fire Test," *New Republic,* IX (November 25, 1916), 93 - 96.

4. Briand, p. 345.

5. Elmer Davis, review of *The Dark River, Saturday Review of Literature,* XVIII (June 25, 1938), 6.

6. "Maki's Perfect Day," *Harper's,* CLIV (March 1927), 421 - 26.

7. *No More Gas* (Boston, 1940), p. 109. Subsequent quotations, with page numbers in parentheses, are from this edition.

8. Ellery Sedgwick, "James Norman Hall," *Atlantic,* CLXXXVIII (September 1951), 21.

9. *The Friends* (Muscatine, Iowa, 1939), p. 23. Subsequent quotations, with page numbers in parentheses, are from this edition.

Chapter Eight

1. *Doctor Dogbody's Leg* (Boston, 1940), p. 297. Subsequent quotations, with page numbers in parentheses, are from this edition.

2. *Oh Millersville!* (Muscatine, Iowa, 1940), p. 14. Subsequent quotations, with page numbers in parentheses, are from this edition. In the list of Hall's books prefacing *My Island Home,* the title is given as *O, Millersville!* On the cover and title page of the first edition, however, the title appears as *Oh Millersville!*

3. "Fern Gravel," *Atlantic,* CLXXVIII (September 1946), 112 - 14.

Chapter Nine

1. *Under a Thatched Roof* (Boston, 1942), p. 6. Subsequent quotations, with page numbers in parentheses, are from this edition.

2. *Men Without Country* (Boston, 1942), p. 56. Subsequent quotations, with page numbers in parentheses, are from this edition.

3. Richard Match, review of *Lost Island, New York Times,* May 28, 1944, p. 6; Diana Trilling, review of *Lost Island, Nation,* CLVIII (June 24, 1944), 742.

4. Match, p. 6.

5. *Lost Island* (Boston, 1944)), p. 48. Subsequent quotations, with page numbers in parentheses, are from this edition.

6. Quoted by Hall in "Frisbie of Danger Island," *The Forgotten One and Other True Tales of the South Seas,* pp. 233 - 34.

Chapter Ten

1. *A Word for His Sponsor: A Narrative Poem* (Boston, 1949), p. 20.

Subsequent quotations, with page numbers in parentheses, are from this edition.

2. *My Island Home*, p. 334.

3. *The Far Lands* (Boston, 1950), p. 1. Subsequent quotations, with page numbers in parentheses, are from this edition.

4. "Death on an Atoll," *Atlantic*, CXLVII (March 1931), 303 - 16.

5. *The Forgotten One and Other True Tales of the South Seas* (Boston, 1952), p. 134. Subsequent quotations, with page numbers in parentheses, are from this edition.

6. *Newsweek*, XL (November 3, 1952), 111. On the other hand, Robert Payne—in a review entitled "A Troubled and Uncomfortable Life," in *Saturday Review of Literature*, LXIII (January 10, 1953), 13—made the incredible assertion that Hall wrote of his boyhood days "with no particular affection, and no horror either." But, unlike most reviewers or for that matter most people who knew Hall personally, Payne did not find Hall an appealing figure but rather "a man with a curious remoteness, a sense of incompleteness, and an almost terrifying mask." The anonymous reviewer in the *New Yorker*, however, believed *My Island Home* to be "infused with the kindly, unassuming personality of its author"—XXVII (December 27, 1952), 66. William McFee in the *New York Herald Tribune Book Review*, October 19, 1952, p. 3, wrote of Hall and his autobiography: "But the character of the man himself shines serenely, a gentle spirit of flawless integrity." And, in the *San Francisco Chronicle*, October 22, 1952, p. 27, J. H. Jackson maintained that in *My Island Home* Hall's character and personality "showed through." Jackson then proceeded to observe: "Here, writing, is that rare human being, a man of good will."

7. *My Island Home: An Autobiography* (Boston, 1952), pp. 328 - 29. Subsequent quotations, with page numbers in parentheses, are from this edition.

Chapter Eleven

1. Murray D. Welch, "James Norman Hall: Poet and Philosopher," *South Atlantic Quarterly*, XXIX (April 1940), 140 - 50. Briand and Johnson have already been cited.

2. Jean Simon, *La Polynésie dans l'art et la littérature de l'occident* (Paris, 1939).

3. James Baird, *Ishmael: A Study of the Symbolic Mode in Primitivism* (Baltimore, 1956), pp. 124 - 25.

4. Lionel Trilling, *The Liberal Imagination: Essays on Literature and Society* (New York, 1950), p. 301.

Selected Bibliography

PRIMARY SOURCES

1. Manuscripts
Hall's papers—including personal correspondence and typescripts of most of his books, essays, and stories—are in the Burlington Library of Grinnell College.

2. Books by James Norman Hall
Kitchener's Mob: The Adventures of an American in Kitchener's Army. Boston: Houghton Mifflin Company, 1916.
High Adventure: A Narrative of Air Fighting in France. Boston: Houghton Mifflin Company, 1918.
On the Stream of Travel. Boston: Houghton Mifflin Company, 1926.
Mid-Pacific. Boston: Houghton Mifflin Company, 1928.
Flying With Chaucer. Boston: Houghton Mifflin Company, 1930.
Mother Goose Land. Boston: Houghton Mifflin Company, 1930.
The Tale of a Shipwreck. Boston: Houghton Mifflin Company, 1934.
The Friends. Muscatine, Iowa: The Prairie Press, 1939.
Doctor Dogbody's Leg. Boston: Atlantic Monthly Press—Little, Brown and Company, 1940.
Gravel, Fern [pseud.]. *Oh Millersville!* Muscatine, Iowa: The Prairie Press, 1940.
Under a Thatched Roof. Boston: Houghton Mifflin Company, 1942.
Lost Island. Boston: Atlantic Monthly Press—Little, Brown and Company, 1944.
A Word for His Sponsor: A Narrative Poem. Boston: Atlantic Monthly Press—Little, Brown and Company, 1949.
The Far Lands. Boston: Atlantic Monthly Press—Little, Brown and Company, 1950.
The Forgotten One and Other True Tales of the South Seas. Boston: Atlantic Monthly Press—Little, Brown and Company, 1952.
Her Daddy's Best Ice Cream. Honolulu: The Advertiser Press Co., Ltd., 1952.
My Island Home: An Autobiography. Boston: Atlantic Monthly Press—Little, Brown and Company, 1952.

3. Books by Charles B. Nordhoff and James Norman Hall
The Lafayette Flying Corps. Boston: Houghton Mifflin Company, 1920.

Faery Lands of the South Seas. New York: Harper & Brothers, 1921.
Falcons of France: A Tale of Youth and the Air. Boston: Atlantic Monthly
   Press—Little, Brown and Company, 1929.
Mutiny on the Bounty. Boston: Atlantic Monthly Press—Little, Brown and
   Company, 1932.
Men Against the Sea. Boston: Atlantic Monthly Press—Little, Brown and
   Company, 1934.
Pitcairn's Island. Boston: Atlantic Monthly Press—Little, Brown and Com-
   pany, 1934.
The Hurricane. Boston: Atlantic Monthly Press—Little, Brown and Com-
   pany, 1936.
The Dark River. Boston: Atlantic Monthly Press—Little, Brown and Com-
   pany, 1938.
No More Gas. Boston: Atlantic Monthly Press—Little, Brown and Com-
   pany, 1940.
Botany Bay. Boston: Atlantic Monthly Press—Little, Brown and Company,
   1941.
Men Without Country. Boston: Atlantic Monthly Press—Little, Brown and
   Company, 1942.
The High Barbaree. Boston: Atlantic Monthly Press—Little, Brown and
   Company, 1945.

4. Contributions by Hall to periodicals (this list omits serializations of Hall's
books)
"Fifth Avenue in Fog," *Century*, LXXXVII (February 1914), 622.
"Charwoman," *Bellman*, XVI (June 6, 1914), 713.
"October," *Boston Transcript*, October 5, 1914, p. 9.
"National Defense," *Outlook*, CXI (November 3, 1915), 538 - 39.
"August Night," *Survey*, XXXVI (August 12, 1916), 498.
"Out of Flanders," *Atlantic*, CXVIII (October 1916), 478 - 80.
"English Opinion as to America," *Outlook*, CXIV (November 1, 1916),
   515 - 18.
"Poetry Under the Fire Test," *New Republic*, IX (November 25, 1916), 93 -
   96.
"The City," *Overland Monthly*, LXVIII (November 1916), 405.
"A Finger and a Huge, Thick Thumb," *Century*, XCIII (January 1917),
   429 - 31.
"From Manhattan," *Overland Monthly*, LXIX (April 1917), 335.
"The Unromantic English," *Outlook*, CXVI (July 18, 1917), 443 - 44.
"Carnot's Story," *Atlantic*, CXX (October 1917), 453 - 62.
"The Splintered Wing," *U.S. Air Service*, II (October 1919), 11 - 12.
"Sir John, Miss Amy, Joseph and Charles," *Atlantic*, CXXIX (June 1922),
   744 - 54.
"The Land Very Far Away," *Woman's Home Companion*, XLIX
   (November 1922), 11 - 12.

"Settling Down in Polynesia," *Woman's Home Companion*, L (May 1923), 12.

"Reminiscences of a Middle-Western School," *Atlantic*, CXXXI (June 1923), 735 - 40.

"Some Polynesian Grandmothers," *Woman's Home Companion*, L (June 1923), 25.

"Narrative of a Journey," *Harper's*, CXLVIII (December 1923), 85 - 96.

"An Autumn Sojourn in Iceland," *Harper's*, CLXVIII (January 1924), 186 - 98.

"The Forgotten One," *Atlantic*, CXXXV (March 1925), 298 - 306.

"Snow Bound," *Atlantic*, CXXXV (April 1925), 447 - 56.

"Memoir of a Laundry Slip," *Harper's*, CL (April 1925), 560 - 70.

"Onward, Christian Soldiers," *Atlantic*, CXXXVI (July 1925), 19 - 32.

"Sing: A Song of Sixpence," *Atlantic*, CXXXVI (December 1925), 726 - 36.

"The Enchantment of the Icelandic Wild," *Travel*, XLVI (February 1926), 26 - 27.

"Why I Live in Tahiti," *Atlantic*, CXXXVII (April 1926), 461 - 68.

"Small Memories," *Atlantic*, CXXXVIII (October 1926), 460 - 68.

"Occupation: Journalist," *Harper's*, CLIII (November 1926), 670 - 84.

"On the Island of Happy Indolence," *Travel*, XLIX (July 1927), 7 - 11.

"Cacoethes Scribendi," *Atlantic*, CXLI (January 1928), 42 - 46.

"Winter Sojourn in Iceland," *St. Nicholas*, LV (March 1928), 343 - 48.

"Fame for Mr. Beatty," *Tanager*, IV (May 1929), 137 - 43.

"To the Ice Mountains," *Atlantic*, CXLIV (July 1929), 20 - 28.

"Escape De Luxe," *Harper's*, CLX (December 1929), 91 - 103.

"Concerning Trains," *Harper's*, CLXI (July 1930), 154 - 58.

"From a Tahitian Commonplace Book," *Virginia Quarterly Review*, VI (October 1930), 557 - 63.

"Still Small Voice," *Atlantic*, CXLVI (December 1930), 714 - 18.

"Death on an Atoll," *Atlantic*, CXLVII (March 1931), 306 - 16.

"The Art of Loafing," *Atlantic*, CXLVIII (July 1931), 51 - 63.

"Youth in These Days," *Harper's*, CLXIII (October 1931), 549.

"Three Books Re-Read: Don Quixote; Mr. Santayana's Soliloquies in England; Charles Lamb's Letters," *Atlantic*, CXLVIII (December 1931), 731 - 32.

"A Starry Night at Arué," *Atlantic*, CXLIX (May 1932), 561.

"At Forty-Five," *Atlantic*, CL (September 1932), 350 - 57.

"Return to Flanders," *Atlantic*, CL (September 1932), 307.

"Too Many Books," *Atlantic*, CL (October 1932), 458 - 60.

"The Coconut Palm" *Atlantic*, CL (October 1932), 510 - 11.

"In a Library," *Harper's*, CLXV (October 1932), 551.

"Happy Endings," *Harper's*, CLXVI (January 1933), 250 - 52.

"Lord of Marutea: The Director's Story," *Atlantic*, CLI (January 1933), 12 - 27.

"Skip: A Strong Icelandic Noun," *Atlantic*, CLI (February 1933), 221 - 26.

"Captain Nicklemagnet and the Gangsters," *Harper's*, CLXVI (February 1933), 377 - 79.
"Comments for Books: For Ben Jonson's Complete Works, in One Volume; For Haydon's Autobiography; For Wordsworth's Lyrical Poems; For . . . , by J. N. H.," *Bookman*, LXXVI (February 1933), 118 - 20.
"The Lives that Authors Lead," *Bookman*, LXXVI (March 1933), 219 - 21.
"The State of Being Bored," *Atlantic*, CLI (March 1933), 318 - 21.
"The Voice," *Atlantic*, CLI (May 1933), 578 - 81.
"Spirit of Place," *Atlantic*, CLII (October 1933), 478 - 83.
"Coral Island," *Rotarian*, XLIII (November 1933), 16 - 17.
"Expatriates," *American Review*, V (May 1935), 185 - 90.
"Wartime Verses and Peacetime Sequel: Airman's Rendezvous: Afterword," *Atlantic*, CLV (May 1935), 563 - 65.
"In Memoriam: The Old Brown Hen," *Atlantic*, CLV (June 1935), 759.
"December in the Tropics," *Atlantic*, CLVII (April 1936), 500.
"Reflections While Worming," *Saturday Review of Literature*, XIV (August 22, 1936), 12 - 13.
"Evening on a Coral Island: Comfort That Turned Cold," *Atlantic*, CLIX (April 1937), 448, 501.
"In Memoriam: Third Ypres," *Harper's*, CLXXV (November 1937), 595.
"Happiness," *Atlantic*, CLXIV (November 1939), 696 - 97.
"Tour de l'île," *Atlantic*, CLXVII (May 1941), 614 - 16.
"My Conrad," *Atlantic*, CLXIX (May 1942), 583 - 87.
"A Word for the Essayist," *Yale Review*, XXXII (September 1942), 50 - 58.
"The Whistle of the Evening Train," *Reader's Digest*, XLII (March 1943), 69 - 72.
"Mr. Bolton's Birthday," *Atlantic*, CLXXIII (June 1944), 70 - 72.
"Reading and Meditating: E. A. Robinson's Poems; S. O. Jewett's Stories; M. Beerbohm's Essays; R. Frost's Poems; When I Am Old," *Atlantic*, CLXXIV (September 1944), 57 - 60.
"Fern Gravel," *Atlantic*, CLXXVIII (September 1946), 112 - 14.
"The G-Note Road," *Atlantic*, CLXXXIV (July 1949), 62 - 65.
"Frisbie of the South Seas," *Atlantic*, CLXXXIV (August 1949), 23 - 32; (September 1949), 63 - 71; (October 1949), 60 - 66.
"Haunted Island," *Saturday Evening Post*, CCXXIII (October 21, 1950), 40 - 41.

SECONDARY SOURCES

BAIRD, JAMES. *Ishmael: A Study of the Symbolic Mode in Primitivism.* Baltimore: John Hopkins University Press, 1956. A scholarly study of Melville containing references to Nordhoff and Hall.
[BARROW, SIR, JOHN]. *The Eventful History of the Mutiny and Piratical Seizure of H. M. S. Bounty: Its Causes and Consequences.* London: John Murray, 1831. A major source for the *Bounty* trilogy. A superb and well-balanced account of the mutiny and its aftermath.

BEECHEY, FREDERICK WILLIAM. *Narrative of a Voyage to the Pacific and Beering [sic] Strait.* London: H. Colburn and R. Bentley, 2 vols., 1831. Most detailed early source for events on Pitcairn.

BREIT, HARVEY. *The Writer Observed.* New York: World Publishing Co., 1956. Account of an interview with Hall.

BRIAND, PAUL L., JR. *In Search of Paradise: The Nordhoff-Hall Story.* New York: Duell, Sloan & Pearce, 1966. Indispensable dual biography of the team.

CONRAD, BARNABY. *Tahiti.* New York: The Viking Press, 1962. Photographs of Hall and his wife and brief comments about him.

FURNAS, J. C. *Anatomy of Paradise: Hawaii and the Islands of the South Seas.* New York: William Sloane Associates, 1948. Iconoclastic book about the South Seas with a few denigrating references to the Nordhoff and Hall novels.

JOHNSON, ROBERT LELAND. *The American Heritage of James Norman Hall: The Woodshed Poet and Co-Author of Mutiny on the Bounty.* Philadelphia: Dorrance & Company, 1969. Provides valuable information about Hall's family and early milieu.

LOVEMAN, AMY. "Everyman's Dilemma," *Saturday Review of Literature,* XXXIV (July 21, 1951), 14. Argues that Hall's South Sea no longer exists.

McCONNAUGHEY, JAMES. "By Nordhoff and Hall," *Saturday Evening Post,* CCX (April 23, 1938), 12, 13, 76, 78, 81, 82. Sketches of the two authors.

MICHENER, JAMES A. *Return to Paradise.* New York: Random House, 1951. Contains scattered references to and comments upon Hall.

OLIVER, DOUGLAS L. *The Pacific Islands.* Revised edition. Garden City, New York: Anchor Books—Doubleday & Company, 1961. Praises Hall's *Lost Island* in a footnote.

SEDGWICK, ELLERY. *The Happy Profession.* Boston: Atlantic Monthly Press—Little, Brown and Company, 1946. This autobiography of Hall and Nordhoff's mentor, editor of the *Atlantic,* contains vivid portraits of both men.

————. "James Norman Hall," *Atlantic,* CLXXXVIII (September 1951), 19 - 21. A posthumous tribute to Hall.

SHAPIRO, HARRY L. *The Heritage of the Bounty: The Story of Pitcairn through Six Generations.* New York: Simon & Schuster, 1936. Study of Pitcairn Island by a noted anthropologist; contains references to Hall.

SHILLIBEER, J. A. *A Narrative of the Briton's Voyage to Pitcairn Island.* London: Law and Whittaker, 1817. Important early source about Pitcairn Island.

SIMON, JEAN. *La Polynésie dans l'art et la littérature de l'occident.* Paris: Boivain et cie, 1939. A few references to Nordhoff and Hall.

SMITH, WALTER G. "James Norman Hall," *Atlantic,* CLXXXVIII (October 1951), 22. Account of Hall's funeral.

SUTTON, HORACE. "Day on Bounty Bay," *Saturday Review of Literature,*

XXXIX (July 14, 1956), 25 - 26. Account of an interview with Hall's
widow.

ULLMAN, JAMES RAMSEY. *Where the Bong Tree Grows: The Log of One
Man's Journey in the South Pacific.* Cleveland: World Publishing
Company, 1963. Rambling, impressionistic travel book with references
to Hall.

VAN GELDER, ROBERT. *Writers and Writing.* New York: Charles Scribner's
Sons, 1946. Account of an interview with Hall.

WEEKS, EDWARD. *In Friendly Candor.* Boston: Atlantic Monthly Press—Little, Brown and Company, 1959. Autobiography by Sedgwick's assis-
tant; contains valuable information about the writing and editing of
the Nordhoff and Hall novels.

WELCH, MURRAY D. "James Norman Hall: Poet and Philosopher," *South
Atlantic Quarterly,* XXIX (April 1940), 140 - 50. Contends Hall's
shorter works are undeservedly neglected and stresses Hall's advocacy
of solitude and reverie.

Index